Jeanne,

Make it,
predictable!

Mary

2016

D0464243

PRAISE FOR *PREDICTABLE PROSPECTING*

Most of what has been written for salespeople about prospecting and pipeline management does nothing to improve their sales results. Either it's too theoretical, which makes it complex and impractical or, even worse, it's too simple to help in the real world. This is the Goldilocks of prospecting books. It walks a just-right balance, with useful cases and examples.

—**Neil Rackham,** bestselling author of *SPIN Selling*

Prospecting is the most important work in sales. It's also the one activity that virtually all salespeople and sales organizations struggle to do consistently. In *Predictable Prospecting* you'll learn how to streamline your prospecting activities into an effective selling system that works! If you're ready to make more money and accelerate your sales productivity, then this book is essential reading.

—**Jeb Blount,** CEO of Sales Gravy, Inc., and author of
Fanatical Prospecting and *People Buy You*

Marylou is one of the finest and brightest minds I know when it comes to "upping the game." She makes outbound prospecting far more productive, predictable, and profitable. Her latest thinking is not only worthwhile reading, it's a MUST if your business goal is increased revenue performance.

—**Jay Abraham,** founder and CEO of
Abraham Group, Inc., and author of
Getting Everything You Can Out of All You've Got

Predictable Prospecting does for the "modern seller" what *Predictable Revenue* did back in its day. In this book you get an updated process that integrates with what is currently working in your playbook. Not a rip-and-replace strategy . . . just better.

—**Trish Bertuzzi,** CEO of The Bridge Group and
author of *The Sales Development Playbook*

Predictable Prospecting offers a great mix of tactical recommendations within a strategic methodology for predictable pipeline generation. This is a great book for staying current on the technologies and processes that are proving to be the most effective.

—**Brent Holloway,** VP of Corporate Sales at
Talend, Inc., and coauthor of *Sales 2.0*

Most sales organizations suffer from an unoptimized sales process. The result? Inconsistent sales and revenue as well as missed forecasts. In *Predictable Prospecting*, Tyler and Donovan show you how to reengineer your sales prospecting into an opportunity machine.

—**Max Altschuler,** founder and CEO of Sales Hacker, Inc.,
and author of *Hacking Sales*

This book is my team's go-to playbook for generating predictable revenue.

—**Paul Fifield,** Chief Revenue Officer of UNiDAYS

Marylou Tyler combines great wisdom and knowledge to help solve the pipeline development challenge we face daily. This book will unlock the door to consistent and predictable pipeline growth like never before.

—**Nick Scaglione,** VP of Sales and Business
Development at VoxGen

This book leads you to a true understanding of sales productivity.

—**Mark Kosoglow,** VP of Sales at Outreach SaaS

PREDICTABLE
PROSPECTING

PREDICTABLE PROSPECTING

HOW TO RADICALLY

INCREASE YOUR

B2B SALES

PIPELINE

MARYLOU TYLER
JEREMEY DONOVAN

New York Chicago San Francisco Athens London Madrid
Mexico City Milan New Delhi Singapore Sydney Toronto

1 2 3 4 5 6 7 8 9   DOC   21 20 19 18 17 16

ISBN: 978-1-259-83564-3
MHID: 1-259-83564-2

e-ISBN: 978-1-259-83565-0
e-MHID: 1-259-83565-0

Library of Congress Cataloging-in-Publication Data

Names: Tyler, Marylou, author. | Donovan, Jeremey, author.
Title: Predictable prospecting : how to radically increase your B2B sales pipeline / Marylou Tyler and
    Jeremey Donovan.
Description: New York : McGraw-Hill, [2016]
Identifiers: LCCN 2016016258 (print) | LCCN 2016025265 (ebook) | ISBN 9781259835643 (alk. paper) |
    ISBN 1259835642 | ISBN 9781259835650 ()
Subjects: LCSH: Industrial marketing. | Sales management.
Classification: LCC HF5415.126 .T945 2016 (print) | LCC HF5415.126 (ebook) | DDC 658.8/04—dc23
LC record available at https://lccn.loc.gov/2016016258

McGraw-Hill Education books are available at special quantity discounts to use as premiums and sales promotions or for use in corporate training programs. To contact a representative, please visit the Contact Us pages at www.mhprofessional.com.

To my parents, who taught me
never to stop learning
—MLT

To my GLG colleagues
—JD

CONTENTS

FOREWORD

In 2011, Marylou and I published *Predictable Revenue: Turn Your Business into a Sales Machine with the $100 Million Best Practices of Salesforce.com*, which was referred to by *Inc.* magazine[1] and others as "the sales bible of Silicon Valley." That book revealed how I created the outbound prospecting program at Salesforce.com and introduced several breakthrough ideas for adding qualified opportunities at the front end of the pipeline in a way that ensures rapid and consistent revenue growth.

The first breakthrough idea was that organizations need to have dedicated prospectors to get off the revenue roller coaster. Blowing out quotas some months and bombing during others is a natural consequence of asking salespeople to do everything—prospecting, qualifying, closing, servicing, and managing accounts. Even the greatest of the great, people who excel at both prospecting and closing, will end up on the roller coaster. It is almost impossible for a single salesperson to balance prospecting and closing in a way that delivers consistent results. To get predictability in revenue, you have to have predictability in lead generation. The way to achieve that is by having dedicated prospectors who feed experienced closers.

The second breakthrough idea was that phone- and e-mail-based outbound prospecting is the most predictable way to create qualified appointments. This concept remains particularly heretical with gurus espousing that the road to riches is paved with inbound marketing and social selling. I too would like to make money while I sleep, but I know sales accrue to salespeople who work the hardest and the smartest.

When *Predictable Revenue* was published, many sales leaders operationalized it by developing phone scripts and e-mail templates as well as measuring the volume of e-mails and dials per day or the number of appointments set. What people miss is the fact that success is not solely about templates and activity. Building a predictable pipeline requires diligent implementation of an end-to-end system. The system starts by finding the right targets and, critically, avoiding the wrong ones. After that, you move the right prospects through an increasingly personalized assembly line toward a final outcome—they buy or they don't.

Before I created the outbound prospecting system at Salesforce .com, I read countless books on sales prospecting, and almost all of them were a waste of time. Most sales books rehash the same high-level ideas over and over again, albeit with new, trademarked names. What made *Predictable Revenue* successful was one strategic concept supported by a few simple, highly actionable tactics that most types of companies could employ. And that same formula is what will make *Predictable Prospecting* indispensable. For starters, Marylou and Jeremey have enhanced the strategic concept. While outbound prospecting remains the big idea, they acknowledge the world has moved from spray and pray to *account-based sales development* (ABSD). In addition, they have taken the tactical elements of *Predictable Revenue* and added pressure-tested details to explain precisely how to build and operate a successful outbound prospecting program. Nothing like this book has existed before.

Each year, outbound prospecting gets more complicated; there are more data sources, more apps, and more tasks. All of this complexity has made it exceptionally challenging to build, maintain, and sustain a consistent sales development system. One of my favorite things about this book is that Marylou and Jeremey have decluttered ABSD by coming up with a step-by-step system that *anyone* can implement. Importantly, their system delivers the nitty-gritty with tips on how to move customers through the buying cycle from unaware to aware to interested to evaluating to purchase. And, while I think it's important for you to stay focused on their complete system, I have to admit that I love the line-by-line analysis of sample e-mail templates.

The information in this book is critical to senior sales executives looking to establish an outbound prospecting team, sales managers leading existing teams, or individual salespeople seeking to improve performance. Individual reps, in particular, can implement Marylou and Jeremey's system by scheduling recurring calendar blocks of two or more hours. Without consistent time blocking, nothing else in this book, or any other book, will predictably increase your sales pipeline.

Marylou and Jeremey's follow-up to *Predictable Revenue* goes deeper, making *Predictable Prospecting* a perfect complement. I decided to go higher-level in my latest book, *From Impossible to Inevitable*, by asking: How do successful sales teams achieve and sustain hypergrowth? Underlying this question are many others, including: Why engage in outbound prospecting in the first place? How does it compare to inbound marketing and word-of-mouth? When does it succeed? When does it fail? In the end, I found what matters most is to "nail a niche" of customers who value your offering as a must-have, not merely as a nice-to-have.

I leave you with this universal truth: prospects don't care what you do. They care about what you do *for them*. At its core, prospecting is simply people selling to people. It's not about templates, scripts, and activities. Prospects need to connect with you and to trust you as a partner who is helping them achieve their goals. If you nail a niche, stay organized with the system outlined in this book, and bring your genuine humanity to prospecting, you will outperform everyone else.

—Aaron Ross, bestselling coauthor of
Predictable Revenue and *From Impossible to Inevitable*
and cofounder of Carb.io (Twitter: @motoceo)

ACKNOWLEDGMENTS

Creating a book is very much a team effort. We are indebted to our agent, Jackie Meyer, our "secret" line editor, PJ Dempsey, and to the following individuals on the McGraw-Hill team for the magic they create behind the scenes: Donya Dickerson, Chelsea Van der Gaag, Pattie Amoroso, Cheryl Hudson, and Steve Straus.

We would like to add our special thanks to our editor extraordinaire, Casey Ebro, whose guidance made the book 10 times better after every draft. We are grateful that you took us to task for any logical inconsistencies. And we appreciate your pushing us to make the book more personal even though both of us are wired for process.

Finally, this book would not have been possible had we not been able to stand on the shoulders of giants, including Aaron Ross, Trish Bertuzzi, Jeb Blount, Matthew Dixon, Brent Adamson, Zig Ziglar, Neil Rackham, Stu Heinecke, Mark Roberge, Mike Weinberg, and so many others.

To my clients: inside this book are our secrets, revealed. Twenty-eight years of figuring out how to start conversations consistently with people we don't know. Getting them to buy predictably so that your businesses can scale and grow. In the late 1980s, we tweaked regular mail to improve response rates, then predictive dialers, and now, the Internet. It's an honor and privilege to teach, mentor, fight in the trenches, and emerge victorious with you.

To my business partner, Bob Kelly: you are a superb sales executive and true master of the sales conversation. I hope we continue working together until we both decide the beach (and golf for you) are more fun than crafting e-mail sequences and building buying scenarios.

To my husband, Jeff: Do you know how many cold e-mails you've read, FTRP and AWAF calls you've listened to, and top-of-funnel schematics and drawings you've viewed? And have you ever objected to a "Honey, can I run this by you?" You are a gift to me.

To my beautiful daughter, Nicki: I love your laugh, and it's so incredibly adorable the way you roll your eyes every time I start conversations with people at airports, in restaurants, waiting in line, asking them what they do, how they describe their job, what they like most about it, what their clients are like. I appreciate your allowing me the opportunity to indulge my curiosity and desire to learn and connect. You are my light. You take my breath away.

And finally to you, my dear reader and newfound friend: I'm so happy you picked up this book. You and I, we're in this together. I've done my best to share what I've learned in the 28 years I've spent doing what I love. In these pages, I hope you find the true secret to predictable prospecting.

—MLT

Those who know me well know that I was born, for better or worse, with intellectual wanderlust. Rather than pursue mastery in a single domain, I strive to hit the professional reset button about once every three years. I was incredibly lucky during my 16 years at Gartner Inc. to have a series of extraordinary bosses who understood my personality and allowed me to reinvent myself as I transformed from engineer to analyst (Greg Sheppard) to product developer (Nir Polonsky) to product manager (Ken Davis) to B2B marketer (Michael Yoo). I owe a special thanks to Nir, Ken, and Michael for showing me the McKinsey way of problem solving and people leadership. After Gartner, I reinvented myself yet again as a sales and sales operations leader with the help of Manny Avrimidis, Jamie Conklin, Alexander Saint-Amand, and Giacomo Iacoangeli.

This book is for each of you and for countless others who have invested in my personal and professional development and fueled my growth.

—JDD

Turning the Unpredictable into the Predictable

Just as we were putting the finishing touches on this book, we had the opportunity to interview the highest-performing account executive at a high-growth, business-to-business (B2B) technology company. Our conversation with her went like this:

"Let's schedule an hour-long block so that we can observe how you prospect." We began this way because we like to watch people in action. (If you ask people to tell you what they do, they tell you what they think you want to hear. If you ask people to tell you what they did, they tell you the good parts and skip the bad.)

"Uh . . . well . . . I don't actually do any cold prospecting anymore," she replied.

"Really?"

"Yeah. I did when I joined a couple years ago. Now, most of my calls are warm."

"How so?"

"We sell seats, annual subscriptions, to individual users. Outside of doing quarterly value reviews, I spend most of my time working internal referrals," she answered.

"When was the last time you called on a new logo?" we persisted.

"About six months ago, we did a blitz day. I think I still have the spreadsheet I used . . ." She opened her laptop and started tapping away. "Here it is," she said, turning the screen toward us.

Staring at the spreadsheet, one of us asked, "What does that column labeled 'Activity' indicate?"

"That's a record of what I did." We noticed every cell in that column read "e-mail." She boasted, "It worked really well. I sent out about 50 e-mails, and I got 5 good replies."

"Did you ever reach out again to the other 45, or was it a one-and-done project?"

With a little less bravado, she answered, "One and done. The blitz was over."

This story is the story of almost every B2B salesperson who survives the first two years in a job. At first they work hard as hunters, making painful, proactive phone calls and drafting cold e-mails. After a while, they have a full book of business to service, after which, somewhere along the line, they transition from hunter to farmer. Ultimately, for sales professionals operating purely in account management mode, the three- or four-year mark becomes very dangerous. No matter how well they engage their existing accounts, a certain number of accounts will not renew for any number of reasons. Maybe their main advocate has changed roles or has moved to a new employer. Maybe the competition has built a better mousetrap. Regardless of the reason, the salesperson is inevitably faced with a gap to making his or her quota and a dry pipeline.

This book is designed for sales development professionals and account executives who want to maintain full, predictable pipelines. Broadly speaking, a complete sales training program consists of insight into (1) specific clients and their use cases; (2) the company's products, marketing, competitive positioning, and so on; (3) selling skills such as communication, time management, goal setting, and negotiating; (4) technology platforms, especially customer relationship management (CRM) tools; and (5) sales processes. There are plenty of great books that focus on the first four areas. In this book we delve deeply and exclusively into the *process for filling the top of the sales funnel* because, without that process, there is no predictability.

Content Preview

Part I focuses on targeting. Chapter 1 provides a framework for internalizing a value proposition and competitive position. Chapter 2 helps sales professionals create an Ideal Account Profile (IAP) so that they can target those accounts with the fastest velocity and the highest lifetime value. Skipping or spending too little time defining an IAP is one of the biggest mistakes salespeople make; they pay a dear cost in time wasted on accounts that may never buy. Chapter 3 explores building an Ideal Prospect Persona (IPP) to ensure that salespeople spend their precious time on the right people in the right accounts.

Part II deals with engaging prospects at the beginning of the buying process. Chapter 4 provides valuable templates for phone and e-mail messaging. Chapter 5 reveals multitouch, multichannel techniques for securing first meetings. Chapter 6 provides a simplified method for the qualifying process, the last stage of the top of the funnel. It is here the Predictable Prospecting process ends, leaving the buying process and closing to other experts. We are also conscious of the fact that closing is incredibly context-dependent in modern B2B selling; hence, crafting a predictable closing process is an extreme if not impossible challenge.

Part III circles back around to the continuous improvement of the Predictable Prospecting process. Chapter 7 covers metrics-based optimization so that salespeople and their colleagues can share and evolve best practices. Chapter 8 considers categories of prospecting enablement tools. Chapter 9 covers managing sales development for establishing or effectively leading an outbound prospecting function. Chapter 10 highlights the 12 habits of the most successful sales development representatives (SDRs).

We strongly recommend that you read the chapters of this book in order and resist the temptation to skip around because we have designed each process step to build constructively into the Predictable Prospecting model.

You will notice that open-mindedness is the common theme that runs throughout the book. Prospecting is context-dependent in every imaginable way. Success depends on aligning the product (or service), the seller, and the prospect. Is feature selling, consultative selling, or solution selling best for such alignment? It depends. Is highly customized account-based prospecting better than mass-personalized prospecting? It depends. Our approach is not intended to be evasive but rather to encourage sales professionals to examine and understand their selling context. Yet, we also try to be prescriptive. For example, if a salesperson has a focused territory with a limited number of high-value accounts, then of course account-based prospecting is the correct approach. Similarly, whether to use feature selling versus consultative selling versus solution selling is totally dependent on how individual prospects prefer to buy.

We understand that proactive prospecting is hard, often thankless work intertwined with rejection, but in this book we promise that it can be predictable. Although we can't promise that predictable processing will be effortless, we can promise that it will be simple and straightforward. It can even be a little bit fun if SDRs approach every day as a game by split-testing communication approaches to measure what does and does not work. Now, let's get started.

PART I

TARGET

Internalizing Your Competitive Position

S ales training programs do a decent, if not an excellent, job of covering product and service knowledge, selling skills, sales technology platforms, and company policies. However, at the end of formal training, most sales professionals still lack the confidence and ability they need to hit the ground running because they haven't developed a strong sense of how to position the value of buying from their company rather than from the competition.

The Six-Factor SWOT Analysis

Fortunately, many frameworks used in strategic planning are invaluable for understanding both a company's competitive positioning and its operating environment. The ubiquitous SWOT analysis, short for strengths, weaknesses, opportunities, and threats, is foremost among these frameworks. While there are exceptions, strengths and weaknesses generally relate to factors internal to the company, and opportunities and threats focus on factors external to the company.

Although a salesperson could review a SWOT analysis assembled by company leadership, we maintain that going through the process of building a SWOT analysis is valuable in much the same way as role playing is helpful. Analyzing a situation with others, especially with tenured peers, allows a salesperson to ask meaningful questions and gain deeper understanding. In addition, by going through this process, the sales professional "owns the output." It's this understanding and ownership that make for a strong foundation of confidence.

Most tutorials on conducting a SWOT analysis progress as you would expect. First, strengths are considered, next weaknesses, and so on. While this approach seems logical, it leads to massive blind spots. For instance, brainstorming without sufficient structure allows a number of cognitive biases to rear their ugly heads. A good example is how the *availability bias* causes people to recall and assign more importance to SWOT factors that are either more recent or more emotionally charged. In addition, groupthink rapidly limits the range of factors that are considered. Finally, mental fatigue begins to kick in by the time the process gets to reviewing threats.

Therefore, instead of starting with each SWOT category and then trying to think of factors, we recommend flipping the process and starting with an exhaustive set of factors affecting a company's position and then considering the strengths, weaknesses, opportunities, and threats for each factor. As shown in Figure 1-1, the factors we consider fall into six groups, including the 4 Ps, reputation, internal resources, external forces, trends, and VUCA (volatile, uncertain, complex, and ambiguous) factors. Let's start with an example from a familiar company, Salesforce .com, to illustrate the approach.

FIGURE 1-1   **Six-Factor SWOT Analysis**

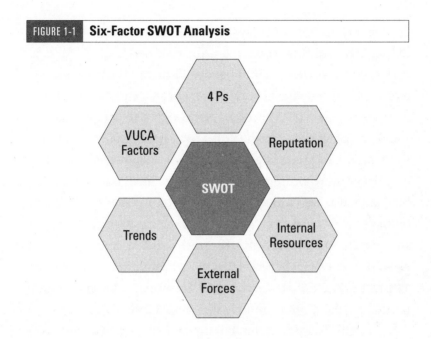

The 4 Ps: Product, Price, Promotion, and Place

In his book *Basic Marketing: A Managerial Approach*, Michigan State University Professor Edmund Jerome McCarthy introduced the 4 Ps marketing mix framework encapsulating the set of strategic decisions a company can make to serve its target market. Published in 1960, the 4 Ps framework has stood the test of time and remains the centerpiece of marketing theory. Conveniently, the 4 Ps also serve as the logical starting point for a SWOT analysis.

Product

The first P includes anything customers can purchase, inclusive of services, whether sold one-off or on a recurring basis. Currently, Salesforce.com has products that include the Sales Cloud for customer relationship management (CRM), the Marketing Cloud for digital marketing automation, and the Service Cloud for help desk support, as well as a number of add-ons and complementary offerings. For the sake of brevity, we will concentrate our SWOT analysis on their CRM product, although a thorough analysis should consider every product offered by the company (or at least every product a given sales professional is empowered to sell).

Strengths: According to Gartner,[1] Salesforce.com is the number one CRM software vendor, with 18.4 percent of the $23 billion worldwide market. Moreover, the company gained market share while formidable competitors such as SAP and Oracle lost ground. From a capability perspective, "References express strong satisfaction with [Salesforce.com's] account, lead, opportunity, product, collaboration, and pipeline management capabilities."[2] Additionally, Salesforce.com has an enviable partner ecosystem in its AppExchange.

Weaknesses: Despite Salesforce.com's increasing market dominance in CRM, users routinely express frustration with the user experience as well as with its underwhelming integration of Microsoft Outlook.

Opportunities: The most obvious opportunities for Salesforce .com are overcoming its weaknesses in the user experience and Outlook integration. Thinking more outside the box, buyers cite[3] functionality as the most important reason for selecting a CRM system. Scanning the competitive landscape as well as customer needs, Salesforce.com has the opportunity to enhance its Sales Cloud with predictive analytics from the acquisition of RelateIQ, customer engagement indicators, and enhanced mobile capabilities.

Threats: We will consider competitive offerings and evolving customer needs as distinct factors later in this SWOT analysis. Here, we force ourselves to think about internal threats to the product. While we cannot get inside Salesforce.com's confidential operations, we can conjecture that the company faces threats from reliability, scalability, and security of its software-as-a-service platform.

Price

This second P is the amount of money given in exchange for goods and services.

Strengths: Though the company has shifted its tagline to "The Customer Success Platform," Salesforce.com is best known for its "No Software" slogan. The original slogan conveys the superior total cost of ownership differentiation for a software-as-a-service model as compared to an on-premises solution requiring software licensing, server infrastructure, and operations personnel.

Weaknesses: With a large installed base, Salesforce.com is extremely limited in its ability to lower prices despite having "the highest-priced cloud SFA [sales force automation] service."[4] Of course, in highly competitive situations and for very large deals, they have granted significant discounts.

Opportunities: Opportunities come with both price increases and price decreases. By adding and subtracting CRM features and functionality, Salesforce.com offers solutions ranging from $25 to $250 per month per user. In addition, the company has the opportunity to expand its customer share-of-wallet by providing and capturing additional value with bundled products and services such as prospect data, customer service solutions, and marketing solutions.

Threats: When the company was founded and during its early existence, its cloud-based delivery model allowed pricing at an attractive per-user discount relative to what it would cost a buyer to install and maintain on-premises solutions from the then-dominant vendors Oracle and SAP. However, with a glut of cloud computing and networking capacity available from the likes of Amazon.com, Google, and IBM, not to mention Oracle's and SAP's own cloud-based CRM solutions, Salesforce.com must now compete on a more even playing field. This is very likely the reason the company is migrating away from its "No Software" pricing message.

Promotion

This third P includes all forms of traditional advertising and digital marketing.

Strengths: In the company's most recent fiscal year,[5] Salesforce .com spent half of its $5.4 billion in total revenue on sales and marketing. While it does not and could not possibly separate the two, it is safe to assume that the company spends 10 to 20 percent of sales, or $500 million to $1 billion, on marketing. Relative to the competition, this is a massive amount, allowing the company to fund a range of activities including, but not limited to, analyst relations, events such as Dreamforce, content marketing via social media and other channels, the company's website, and traditional print and television advertising. In addition to their outbound marketing activity, the company's large installed base of customers is a significant marketing asset.

Weaknesses: Often one's greatest strength is simultaneously one's greatest weakness. The company's very name does not lend itself well to extending into new segments such as customer service and marketing automation. In addition, Salesforce.com, as we mentioned earlier, has wisely decided to shift from its "No Software" slogan to more positive, customer-centric positioning rather than technology-centric messaging.

Opportunities: Marketing messages and channels are constantly evolving. This fact means that Salesforce.com has the opportunity to optimize its existing programs to earn a higher return on investment as measured by increases in brand equity or qualified lead generation. In addition, the company could also explore new marketing tactics, especially in the digital domain.

Threats: Due to changing consumer preferences and an ever-shifting digital landscape, marketing threats are more prevalent than ever. For instance, Google's evolving search algorithms mean Salesforce.com needs to remain hypervigilant with search engine optimization (SEO) to prevent slipping in search engine results page (SERP) rank for valuable, unbranded terms such as "CRM" and "SFA." Turning to consumer preferences, the value of large and small in-person events is declining with the proliferation of information and social media alternatives because of increasingly busy schedules that make getting away from the office harder and harder.

Place

This last P is inclusive of all distribution channels, but it differs in meaning depending on the type of company. For a business-to-consumer (B2C) food and beverage retailer like Starbucks, place includes its ubiquitous stores, tightly controlled partner network operations in hotels and airports, and distribution through wholesalers into grocery stores. For a business-to-business service provider like an advertising agency, place is a combination of the company's direct sales team and its website.

Strengths: Salesforce.com has three strong channels of distribution. Self-service customers can purchase quickly and easily on the company's website. In addition, the company has a large sales organization that includes a field sales team serving larger enterprises and an inside sales team serving small to medium-sized businesses. Complementing their internal efforts, Salesforce.com manages a partner network consisting of thousands of value-added resellers.

Weaknesses: A rapidly growing company like Salesforce.com will inevitably run into bottlenecks adding qualified sales capacity and maintaining sales productivity.

Opportunities: Like most companies, Salesforce.com organizes its sales professionals by geography. However, the company could capitalize by joining the growing trend toward customer-centric organizational structures, and, in particular, organizing by industry segment.

Threats: There are real threats to each of the three distribution channels at Salesforce.com. First, any service disruption to its website would have a negative impact on sales. Second, especially with an expanding number of salespeople, it will naturally face challenges in training and retaining new hires. Third, the company's very large partner ecosystem carries risk if partners are not tightly managed and are allowed to start preferentially recommending competitive solutions or fail to deliver successful implementations.

Table 1-1 provides a condensed representation of the 4 Ps SWOT analysis for Salesforce.com. When conducting a SWOT analysis using the 4 Ps inclusive of the factors we will cover, the goal of a salesperson is not perfection but rather internalization of enough information to be able to convey the company's value proposition and to handle most objections.

Reputation Factors

As with the 4 Ps, reputation factors involving customers and partners tend to be more internal and will, therefore, generate more strengths and weaknesses than opportunities and threats.

When Professor McCarthy developed the 4 Ps model, he put customers at the center of the framework. In the 1960s,

| TABLE 1-1 | 4 Ps SWOT Analysis of Salesforce.com | | | |

	STRENGTHS	WEAKNESSES	OPPORTUNITIES	THREATS
Product	• Market share • Product capabilities • AppExchange	• User experience • Microsoft Outlook integration	• Predictive analytics • Customer engagement indicators • Mobile experience	• Reliability • Scalability • Security
Price	• Low cost relative to on-premises solutions	• High cost relative to other cloud solutions	• Bundling data, customer service functionality, marketing functionality, and so on	• New entrants
Promotion	• Brand recognition • Dreamforce events • Marketing budget	• Company name too narrow	• Digital marketing	• Changes to search engine algorithms • Proliferation of information
Place	• Self-service • Direct sales • Reseller network	• Sales hiring • Sales productivity	• Restructure around industry lines	• Web service disruption • Sales employee retention • Partner quality

companies had a greater degree of control over customer relationships. Back then, mass advertising ruled, and it was extremely difficult for word-of-mouth, good or bad, to spread, unless a business was operating in a very small town. Conversely, in today's hyperconnected world, reputation is viral, persistent, and volatile. Businesses must defend their reputations at all costs. In particular, one irate customer can do enormous damage—just ask United Airlines, which suffered when Dave Carroll posted his song "United Breaks Guitars" on YouTube and garnered more than 15 million views as well as massive press coverage.[6]

One of the best ways to assess reputation is by using the Net Promoter Score (NPS)[7] developed by Fred Reichheld while he was a consultant at Bain & Company. NPS measures customer loyalty by asking, on a scale of 0 to 10, "How likely is it that you would recommend [company X] to a friend or colleague?" To calculate the NPS, which can range from −100 to +100, the percentage of *detractors* (ratings of 0 to 6) is subtracted from the percentage of *promoters* (ratings of 9 or 10). The percentage of *passives* (ratings of 7 or 8) is ignored. Average Net Promoter Scores vary wildly by industry, ranging from the high 40s for auto dealers (yes, really) to low single digits for television service providers (no surprise there).[8] With an NPS routinely in the low 80s, USAA, a financial services provider for the military community and their families, sits at the pinnacle of customer loyalty year after year.

Customer Reputation

Now, let's return to our detailed exploration of Salesforce.com by considering its customer reputation.

Strengths: While the company no longer routinely discloses its customer renewal rate, it has historically stood in the mid-80s, considered excellent for a B2B service provider. (B2B service renewal rates of above 80 percent are excellent, 70 to 80 percent are good, and below 70 percent are poor.) While one could argue that Salesforce.com's customers are locked in, the combination of market share growth and fairly steady retention rates is a good sign that most customers are satisfied with the company. Additionally, the company has a strong reputation for corporate social responsibility as demonstrated by its 1-1-1 model: employees are given 1 percent of their time (6 days per employee per year) to devote to volunteer work, and the company donates or discounts 1 percent of products to nonprofits and allocates 1 percent of equity to nonprofits.

Weaknesses: Average Net Promoter Scores for enterprise software vendors are typically around 30. According to the Temkin Group, an independent customer experience research firm, the NPS for Salesforce.com was stable in the 63rd percentile among firms measured in 2012[9] and 2013.[10] However, the company's NPS dropped to the 29th percentile in 2014.[11] (*Note:* The percentiles given are *not* Net Promoter Scores. Companies that maintain Net Promoter Scores above the 50th percentile for the long term are expected to gain market share. The only publicly available NPS for Salesforce.com from the Temkin Group is a score of 34 in 2012, which was slightly above average among major technology vendors.)

Opportunities: While Salesforce.com gets high marks from sales leadership because the solution provides visibility into pipeline and performance, frontline salespeople are less enamored. Their main complaint is that Salesforce.com is exactly like every CRM tool—an onerous data entry and activity tracking system that only slows them down. Salesforce.com's dated user experience does not help. To that end, the company's biggest opportunity to enhance its customer reputation lies with overhauling its user interface, and the company is actively working on that, beginning with its winter 2015 release of the "Lightning" experience.

Threats: Customer reputation is under constant attack. Salesforce.com faces reputation threats from service outages, botched implementations (even if caused by third parties), and radical changes to the user interface.

A final note on customer considerations before we transition from customer reputation to partner considerations: it's important to understand that while we took a 1,000-foot view of Salesforce.com's customer reputation, the context in which an individual salesperson operates is what matters. By context, we mean the breadth of a salesperson's product portfolio and the scope—industry, geography, job role, job level, company size, and so on—of his or her territory.

Partner Reputation

When discussing product strengths, we touched upon the importance of partner reputation for Salesforce.com.

Strengths: Again, with its dominant partner ecosystem of thousands of application developers and value-added resellers, the company devotes significant resources of training, certification, tools, online communities, support, and events to enable these partners.

Weaknesses: Salesforce.com risks alienating its third-party application developers as it integrates greater functionality into its core platform. Similarly, as the company expands the capacity of its sales team, it will likely encroach upon the products and services of its value-added reseller (VAR) partners.

Opportunities: The AppExchange ecosystem offers a virtuous circle: the more partners, the more customers there are; the more customers, the more partners there are. The company should make every effort to grow its partner network, particularly by supporting application developers.

Threats: The dark side of growth is dilution. Salesforce.com must avoid the temptation to increase margin by underinvesting in its partner network as its business expands.

Table 1-2 provides a condensed reputation factor SWOT analysis of Salesforce.com.

TABLE 1-2	**Reputation Factor SWOT Analysis of Salesforce.com**

	STRENGTHS	WEAKNESSES	OPPORTUNITIES	THREATS
Customer Reputation	• High renewal rate • Corporate social responsibility	• Declining Net Promoter Score	• Improve user experience	• Service outages • Third-party implementation failures
Partner Reputation	• Strong application developer and VAR ecosystem	• Risk of alienating certain partners as they add features	• Grow partner network, especially app developers	• Underinvestment in partner ecosystem

Internal Resource Factors

A thorough SWOT analysis evaluates four pools of internal resources:

- The first pool, financial resources, includes cash on hand as well as access to capital.

- The second pool, intellectual property, includes patents as well as trade secrets in the form of internal processes and tools. In addition, data has become an increasingly valuable component of intellectual capital.

- The third pool, human capital, includes employee knowledge and skills as well as culture and leadership capability. In our ultratransparent world, employer reputation has become a key human capital asset or liability.

- The fourth and final pool, physical assets, includes facilities, equipment, and natural resources. For brevity, we will touch on only a few of the most important factors for Salesforce .com's SWOT analysis.

Strengths: As measured by Glassdoor, Salesforce.com gets high marks (4.0 out of 5.0) for providing good work-life balance and the opportunity to work with smart people. In addition, 78 percent of reviewers would recommend a job at Salesforce.com to a friend. What's more, CEO Marc Benioff has an impressive 94 percent approval rating.

Weaknesses: The $1 billion in cash held by Salesforce.com pales in comparison to the war chests of many large technology vendors who may use their financial muscle to compete with or acquire the company.

Opportunities: As data center capacity becomes more of a commodity, Salesforce.com has the opportunity to improve performance and lower costs by partnering with a third-party vendor such as Amazon.com, IBM, or Google.

Threats: Salesforce.com is likely to face more frequent intellectual property (IP) challenges as it expands its business into new areas beyond sales force automation despite having more than 1,000 patents and access to 40,000 more via its agreement with Intellectual Vendors.[12]

Table 1-3 provides a condensed resource factor SWOT analysis of Salesforce.com.

TABLE 1-3	**Resource Factor SWOT Analysis of Salesforce.com**			
	STRENGTHS	WEAKNESSES	OPPORTUNITIES	THREATS
Financial		• Cash low relative to major competitors		
Intellectual Property				• Low IP outside of sales automation
Human Capital	• Employee satisfaction			
Physical Assets			• Outsource data center	

External Forces

Harvard Business School Professor Michael Porter's Five Forces framework—the classic approach to analyzing the attractiveness of an industry for purposes of developing competitive strategy—was developed because Professor Porter felt the SWOT analysis framework was too company specific and did not have enough rigor.[13] Nevertheless, we feel the SWOT approach has served us well. In our opinion, it is advantageous to combine the two.

Customer Factors

Our analysis begins with Porter's "bargaining power of buyers," which we call "customer factors."

Strengths: Salesforce.com's Sales Cloud buyers are not individual salespeople but, rather, executive leaders, including heads of sales, CFOs, and CEOs. Large companies have low buyer power because they have few options other than Salesforce.com if they need to rely on a secure, reliable, cloud-based solution from a vendor with significant customer service resources and an extensive partner ecosystem. In addition, financial and monetary switching costs attached to going from one CRM platform to another, including Salesforce.com, are extremely high.

Weaknesses: Buyers employed by small and medium-sized businesses (SMBs) can have enormous market power, access to better pricing, and more advanced functionality if they are willing to compromise on certain Salesforce.com strengths, such as its partner ecosystem.

Opportunities: Salesforce.com can expand the value it creates and captures by investing in its traditional areas of strength as well as by integrating new functionality, including predictive analytics and marketing automation features.

Threats: The more information buyers can access, the greater their bargaining power. Websites like G2Crowd, Quora, TrustRadius, GetApp, and SoftwareAdvice provide a wealth of information on pricing and tactics that customers can tap when negotiating with Salesforce.com.

Competitive Factors

This label of "competitive factors" covers three of Porter's Five Forces—"threat of new entrants," "industry rivalry," and "threat of substitutes." Even though these factors have made their appearance in the Salesforce.com SWOT analysis thus far, we thought it necessary to review briefly a few items that might have gone unnoticed.

Strengths: In its market-leading position, Salesforce.com can afford to invest heavily in its product and its marketing. In addition, on the basis of its large installed base of users and its enviable developer and reseller ecosystem, the company often wins in competitive situations.

Weaknesses: Despite the company's leading position, its competitors collectively control more than 80 percent of the market for CRM solutions. In addition to larger vendors like Oracle and SAP, Salesforce.com is under constant attack by innovative, lower-priced, reasonably well-funded newcomers such as SugarCRM, Zoho, Insightly, Nimble, Infusionsoft, and scores of others. Market leaders have very little desire or ability to lower prices and instead seek to remain competitive by increasing functionality. (Lou Gerstner's decision to drastically lower mainframe prices when he ran IBM is one of the rare exceptions in the technology industry.) As Clayton Christensen outlines in *The Innovator's Dilemma*, dominant vendors face an existential threat when newcomers first dominate a niche and then develop good-enough functionality to serve the masses.

Opportunities: To increase its strength relative to the competition, Salesforce.com should continue to pursue innovation in both pricing and functionality.

Threats: The convergence of sales force automation (SFA) and marketing automation platforms (MAPs) is perhaps the biggest threat to Salesforce.com. This convergence is happening because companies are most successful when they have a multichannel view of their customer and prospect engagement online and offline. Recognizing this threat, the company has made a number of acquisitions, most notably Pardot (for B2B) and ExactTarget (for B2C). The race is on between MAP vendors integrating SFA functionality and SFA vendors integrating MAP functionality; hence, Salesforce.com must make quick work of its own integration efforts.

Bargaining Power of Suppliers

The last of Porter's Five Forces is the "bargaining power of suppliers." Although this is usually a much stronger consideration for companies that manufacture physical goods, service providers also deal with powerful suppliers.

Strengths: As a cloud-based service provider, Salesforce.com builds and maintains large data centers around the world. Fortunately, the markets for servers, networking equipment, and data bandwidth are all highly competitive with low switching costs due to interoperability and with a large pool of world-class suppliers from which to choose.

Weaknesses: The biggest supplier to Salesforce.com is its own labor force. While unionization is unlikely, demand for skilled engineers and sales professionals remains extremely high, especially in the locations where the company operates.

Opportunities: With labor as a major input, any efforts Salesforce.com makes to improve the intrinsic benefits of working for the company will pay dividends, including expanding its commitment to social responsibility and investing in its culture.

Threats: The price of energy used in the company's data centers is increasing due to political instability and diminishing natural resources. In addition, unlike other inputs, switching energy suppliers is not easy and also poses a threat to margin as energy prices rise.

Table 1-4 provides a condensed external forces SWOT analysis of Salesforce.com.

TABLE 1-4	**External Forces SWOT Analysis of Salesforce.com**			
	STRENGTHS	WEAKNESSES	OPPORTUNITIES	THREATS
Customers	• Proven large supplier • High switching costs	• SMBs willing to compromise	• Integrate predictive analytics and marketing automation	• High transparency enabled by software product review websites
Competitors	• Investment in product and marketing • Large installed base • Partner ecosystem	• Highly fragmented market • Limited ability to lower prices	• Pricing innovation • New features	• Convergence of SFA and MAPs
Suppliers	• Highly competitive markets for infrastructure and data services	• Threat of unionization • High demand for engineers and salespeople	• Expand investment in social responsibility	• Rising energy prices

Trends

The two major trend categories are social-demographic and technology. Trends are important because they are the external (macro) factors that affect business success. Trends are different from VUCA factors, which we will delve into next, in that they are long term and are either immediately observable or reasonably certain to occur. Current social-demographic trends include longer lifespans, the rise of millennials, the freelance economy, and climate change. Current technology trends include mobile computing, social collaboration, cloud computing, and big data.

Strengths: Salesforce.com has been positioned to take advantage of all notable technology trends including social collaboration with its Chatter feature, mobile applications, big data analytics with its dashboards, and cloud computing for its operating model.

Weaknesses: No major weaknesses related to social-demographic or technology trends.

Opportunities: If the rise of the freelance economy turns out to be as real as its hype, Salesforce.com has the opportunity to offer solutions to solopreneurs if it can crack the code on a virtually zero-service-needed offering. The company's acquisition of RelateIQ is Salesforce.com's first action to capture this opportunity.

Threats: Climate change will negatively affect Salesforce.com's and its customers' operations with increasing frequency.

VUCA Factors: Volatile, Uncertain, Complex, and Ambiguous Occurrences

The frequency and timing of all VUCA factors are unpredictable by definition. However, these volatile, uncertain, complex, and ambiguous occurrences, while mostly negative and external, such as economic shocks, political instability, acts of terrorism, or natural disasters, can also be internally generated (employment litigation) and positive (economic expansion).

Strengths: We presume that Salesforce.com has business interruption insurance to provide relief from many VUCA factors. In addition, the company makes significant investments to protect itself from digital terrorism.

Weaknesses: No company, Salesforce.com included, can ensure against every negative VUCA factor, nor can any company be positioned to take advantage of every positive VUCA factor.

Opportunities: Salesforce.com should align its geographic footprint with that of its large, multinational customers to take advantage of economic expansion in emerging economies.

Threats: Most of the VUCA factors listed above are threats, and all are risks to Salesforce.com to one degree or another.

Table 1-5 provides a condensed trends and VUCA factor SWOT analysis of Salesforce.com.

TABLE 1-5	**Trends and VUCA Factor SWOT Analysis of Salesforce.com**			
	STRENGTHS	WEAKNESSES	OPPORTUNITIES	THREATS
Trends	• Social collaboration • Mobile • Big data • Cloud computing	• None	• Solopreneur expert economy	• Climate change
VUCA Factors	• Business interruption insurance	• Inability to react to many VUCA factors	• Expansion in emerging economies	• (*See* weaknesses)

Looking back, the SWOT analysis for Salesforce.com produced a *lot*, perhaps even too much, information. Sometimes, the factors even overlapped, which is all right because the next step is to simplify the analysis. We'll do this by first going item by item

FIGURE 1-2	SWOT Analysis for Salesforce.com

STRENGTHS	WEAKNESSES	OPPORTUNITIES	THREATS
1. Number one in the market	1. Dated user experience	1. Expand sales and marketing operations to new geographies	1. Cloud technology and "No Software" message no longer differentiating
2. High customer renewal rate	2. Recent decline in Net Promoter Score	2. Integrate predictive analytics	2. Rising number of strong competitors, both large and small, due to Salesforce.com's success
3. Rich AppExchange with thousands of add-ons and value-added resellers	3. Tight labor supply	3. Integrate marketing automation	
	4. Low penetration in SMBs	4. Outsource data center to noncompetitor	3. Data terrorism
4. Low total cost of ownership	5. Possibility that the Salesforce .com name may not extend well to new categories beyond SFA		4. Increasing energy price volatility
5. Proven commitment to corporate social responsibility			

and assigning each a simple score of high, medium, or low importance in competitive prospecting situations. Next, as shown in Figure 1-2, we'll list the items ranked as high impact in a two-by-two table that fits into a single page as we did in Figure 1-1. Think harder if you have fewer than three items in one of the four boxes, and prioritize more aggressively if you have more than five.

Since companies, industries, and customers are in a constant state of change, we recommend that salespeople review and, if necessary, refresh their SWOT analysis at least once each quarter. The refresh is an ideal team activity so colleagues can share insights and experiences.

We know that we spent a disproportionate amount of time on the SWOT analysis. This was intentional because it is the precursor to the many steps leading to building the Predictable Prospecting model. In the next chapter we will show you how to develop an Ideal Account Profile (IAP).

Developing an Ideal Account Profile

The SWOT analysis we completed in the previous chapter provides sales professionals with the ability to clearly communicate the differentiated value proposition of their company and its products. In the Predictable Prospecting method, you'll learn how to identify those you can successfully approach with that message. This will be done in two steps: deciding on the ideal accounts to target, which is covered in this chapter, and identifying the ideal people to target within those accounts, which is covered in the following chapter.

The maxim "You can't be all things to all people" perfectly expresses the philosophy behind developing an Ideal Account Profile. In reality, even if a company were able to sell its products to every other company on the planet, neither the company nor any individual salesperson could do so without infinite time and infinite energy. The process revealed in this chapter, known as *market segmentation*, is all about maximizing the return on effort by focusing on those companies with both a high lifetime value and a high likelihood of buying.

Market Segmentation

Lifetime value takes into account both sides of the long-term profit equation as well as intangibles. The revenue side of the equation includes factors such as the transaction size, renewal rate, and expansion opportunity. The cost side of the equation includes standard product costs, customer acquisition costs, and service-support costs. In addition to these measurable quantities, signing a particular customer may have enormous intangible benefits, the strongest of which would be the value of the customer as a reference.

While we share a universal framework for building market segments, there is no universal set of segments since every company's situation is unique, even among seemingly direct competitors. Our approach considers segmentation factors in three categories: firmographic fit, operational fit, and situational fit (Figure 2-1). The "fit factors" within these three categories are proxies, to a greater or lesser extent, for customer needs and budget. As such, they function as a coarse mechanism for prioritizing those companies with which to attempt to do business and identifying those to avoid.

An Ideal Account Profile is simply a set of market segments that meet the criteria of high lifetime value and high likelihood of purchasing. We use the word "high" rather than "highest" or "maximum" with intent. A segment with maximum lifetime value and purchasing likelihood could easily be a segment of one. For a set of factors to be usable, those factors need to satisfy certain basic requirements.

First, when applied, the segmentation factors should identify the right number of target companies. Too few companies and the salesperson will not be fully occupied; too many companies and the salesperson will not have enough time to devote the level of activity required to meet his or her goals.

FIGURE 2-1	**Segmentation Factors for an Ideal Account Profile (IAP)**
FIRMOGRAPHIC	• Industry • Size (employees or revenues) • Geography
OPERATIONAL	• Equipment and technology • Purchasing policies • Decision-making process
SITUATIONAL	• Strategic initiatives • Bias toward insourcing versus outsourcing • Financial health • Executive transitions • Value, mission, and culture alignment

Second, the factors should be measureable with reasonable effort. Again, the whole point of developing an Ideal Account Profile is to maximize the return on effort. Focus on factors that are high impact and low cost to obtain and ignore factors that are low impact and high cost. Factors requiring a judgment call are those that are either high impact and high cost or low impact and low cost.

Third, the factors should identify distinct target segments, each possessing a specific set of needs. In addition, distinct segments should be accessible through homogenous communication channels to ensure efficient outreach.

Fourth and final is stability. Market segmentation is a strategic process, and as such changes should be made only over longer time horizons (a year or more) or when the company's overall strategy is in rapid flux (as is often the case in new businesses).

The Fit Factors

These factors include firmographic, operational, and situational characteristics.

Firmographic Fit

Similar to business-to-consumer segmentation based on demographic factors, business-to-business segmentation classically begins with firmographic factors that include industry, company size, and geography. These factors are relatively inexpensive to obtain since the market for business data is quite competitive with long-established providers such as Hoover's and S&P Capital IQ and newer entrants such as ZoomInfo and DiscoverOrg, in addition to scores and scores of other providers.

Industry: If the starting point of market segmentation is firmographic fit, then the starting point of firmographic fit is industry. Currently, there are two standard classification systems: SIC, first established in the United States in 1937 and used internationally, and NAICS, first released in 1997. We'll start with the newer NAICS (last revised in 2012), which was intended to replace SIC. Note that NAICS has 24 active two-digit codes, 312 active four-digit codes, and 1,065 six-digit codes. Familiar two-digit industries include manufacturing, information, and retail trade.

The most useful industry classification is manageable in size (typically 10 or fewer) and includes nonoverlapping combinations of NAICS codes. The set will vary based on your target industries, but a good starting point of 10 items plus an "other" category is as follows (codes in parentheses): education (61); energy and utilities (22); finance and insurance (52); government (92); healthcare (62); information technology (334x, 5112, 518x, 5415); manufacturing (31 to 33 excluding 3254 and 334x); media and entertainment (71); pharmaceutical (3254); and other (11, 21, 23, 42, 44 and 45,

48 and 49, 51 excluding 5112 and 518x, 53, 54 excluding 5415, 55, 56, 72, 81).

Most companies manage a semicustom industry target list aligned with business opportunity. Like our reference example, a given list may go deeper or broader in various segments. We strongly recommend creating an "other" category to hold industries that are a poor fit. As a reminder, each segmentation factor provides a rough way to screen in desirable companies and screen out undesirable ones. Undesirable industries may have little expected demand for a company's products, too much (or too little) regulatory intensity, or poor industry health.

Company size: This is the next most common firmographic fit factor. Since most companies sell to both public and private entities, bands consisting of the number of employees are usually the easiest to deal with. Unfortunately, company size classifications are far less standardized in comparison to industry classifications. Nonetheless, a useful set of categories are as follows (revenue ranges are based on a reasonable, albeit rough, estimate of $500,000 per employee; the number of U.S. headquarters from Hoover's based on revenue):

- *Microbusiness and/or small office or home office:* 10 employees or fewer; up to $5 million; 228,657 companies

- *Small business:* 11 to 100 employees; $5 million to $50 million; 114,187 companies

- *Medium business:* 101 to 1,000 employees; $50 million to $500 million; 23,653 companies

- *Large enterprise:* 1,001 to 10,000 employees; $500 million to $5 billion; 5,119 companies

- *Extra-large enterprise:* More than 10,000 employees; over $5 billion; 983 companies

While the above employee and revenue bands will serve most businesses, the optimal breakpoints can be different for each business. Additionally, employees and revenues may not always be the best measures of size. For example, a business providing secure office-to-office communications services might be more interested in the number of locations, or a company providing facilities services might be more interested in a prospect's total square footage.

There is an old adage in sales that it takes as much effort to win a deal with a large company as it does a small one. If that assumption is correct, then why not just focus on selling to the Fortune 500 or Fortune 1000? As of 2015, all Fortune 500 companies fit in the extra-large enterprise category by revenue ranging from number 1 Walmart at $485 billion to number 500 McGraw-Hill Financial at $5.2 billion. The Fortune 1000 cuts off at E*TRADE Financial with revenue of $2.0 billion. The problem is that it is *actually* easier to sell to smaller companies. Jumbo companies are highly risk averse, and they have many hoops to jump through; it takes only one no to scuttle the deal. Moreover, competition is more intense when trying to sell to a Fortune 1000 company.

Geography: The main considerations surrounding geographic targeting include language, the ability to provide high-quality service, and tax complexity.

With firmographic theory in hand, turn back to the analysis of Salesforce.com. Rob Acker, the executive tasked with lead generation and account management, had pored over the data he had been collecting and noticed that Salesforce.com was experiencing success with small companies having fewer than 30 employees. The value of segmentation is in the results. CEO Mark Benioff confirmed this by saying, "It turned out to be a very good decision to focus more attention on smaller businesses. The close rates were high, and the sales time and cost of sale were low. We experienced phenomenal growth in this area and expanded from 4 sales reps to 20 reps in just six months."

Despite being a cloud-based company and possessing unlimited reach, Salesforce.com also benefited from industry and geographic segmentation. Specifically, the company found early success right in their backyard among high-technology companies in Silicon Valley. Their first customer was Blue Martini Software, a vendor of e-commerce applications for retailers based in San Mateo, California (and a company in which Benioff had previously invested). The second was iSyndicate, a San Francisco–based content syndication provider. The third, the web-hosting provider colo .com, was also based in San Francisco. As Salesforce.com matured, it was able to expand to larger prospects in new industries and wider geographies. Its initial success hinged on starting in a niche, and it has grown over time such that today it is a successful sales organization that, like every successful sales organization, is a harmonious aggregation of countless industry, size, and geographic niches, what sales professionals refer to as "territories."

If segmentation completeness were measureable, firmographic fit would get companies 80 percent of the way to the finish line. Using the 80-20 rule, firmographic fit only takes 20 percent of the effort required to get to 80 percent of the way to an Ideal Account Profile.

Operational Fit

If firmographic fit is too coarse, operational fit is the next set of segmentation factors to consider. This includes everything about a prospect's medium- to long-term business operations, including processes and installed equipment. While some of these operational variables may be available for purchase via a third-party database, most are not and require some degree of discovery. We will explore three common operational fit factors, but each company should investigate only those factors worth the effort for their business.

Current equipment: The first operational fit factor takes into consideration the prospect's current equipment and technology. For instance, consider SalesLoft, whose excellent sales workflow management tool works best when integrated with Salesforce .com. To maximize its return on effort, SalesLoft should segment on companies known to be Salesforce.com users. Similarly, a company that provides spare parts for agricultural equipment would segment farms based on their use of Caterpillar, Case IH, John Deere, New Holland, and so on.

Purchasing policy: This is the second operational fit factor. Imagine selling parts to Boeing for its 787 Dreamliner. From project launch to first delivery, the airplane took over seven years and $32 billion to develop, according to the *Seattle Times*.[1] The plane sells for anywhere between $125 million and $225 million. Boeing's suppliers must deal with long cycle times, extreme quality standards, complex inventory management, and unimaginable insurance indemnification. At Boeing and elsewhere, purchasing policies may contribute to a better or worse fit. This type of purchasing policy also includes, but is not limited to, companies with a preference for leasing rather than ownership, buying from minority-owned businesses, purchasing based on sustainability requirements, or selecting from a Government Services Administration (GSA) price list.

Buying decisions: This third operational fit factor focuses on not just how the prospect company makes buying decisions but whether the company centralizes purchasing within a procurement team or decentralizes to individual business units or branch offices. No single purchasing approach is inherently better or worse from the perspective of a supplier. Centralized purchasing, for example, is a great fit for large, complex orders.

Let's apply each of these three operational fit factors to Salesforce.com, as it relates to two cases: one is a newly formed business, and the other is a large, established enterprise. In the case of the newly formed business, Salesforce.com's fit is excellent since there is no installed base of technology, and new businesses often prefer to use cloud-based solutions where possible to avoid infrastructure purchase and maintenance costs. In the case of the large, established enterprise, Salesforce.com will most likely run into a competitive on-premises CRM solution. Since the switching costs of moving data and retraining sales teams are very high, the prospect must be deeply frustrated either with the functionality or total cost of ownership of their existing solution. Salesforce.com may find more success knocking out certain competitors rather than others; and if that is the case, knowledge of the competitive CRM solution in use will help it prioritize prospect segments to target.

With respect to the second operational fit factor, purchasing policies, Salesforce.com should experience far less friction with either business than a Boeing supplier would, so the company does not need to segment here. Similarly, with buying decisions, it is not worth Salesforce.com's effort for either the new or the established business in this case.

Situational Fit

When firmographic fit and operational fit do not provide sufficiently meaningful target segments, then companies must turn to situational fit. In contrast to operational fit factors, which are medium- to long-term prospect company characteristics, situational fit factors are more opportunistic. As such, they require more effort to ascertain and are more evanescent.

Strategic initiatives: This is often the most fruitful area to find situational fit factors. Since our overarching goal here is efficient segmentation, we are after information that can be gleaned *before* engaging decision makers in conversation. Some of the best sources for this type of information include annual reports and analyst reports. For example, the "Message from our Chairman" section in Boeing's latest annual report[2] highlights the following initiatives to create likely opportunities for a wide range of vendors:

- Under the moniker of "Partnering for Success," Boeing is working to increase quality and reduce costs by asking suppliers for more transparency into their manufacturing processes and financial statements.

- To control development costs, Boeing is standardizing its product development process. In addition, the company is working to adopt common parts across its products.

- Boeing is investing in safety standards, tools, and equipment to reduce serious injuries.

- To reduce the company's environmental footprint, Boeing is investing in a range of options, including renewable energy, sustainable aviation biofuel, and airplane noise reduction technology.

Internal capabilities or the propensity to insource or outsource: This second situational fit factor complements the analysis of a prospect's strategic initiatives. For instance, Boeing may consider its product development process to be a source of competitive advantage and may not, therefore, look to outside consulting or training organizations for assistance. On the other hand, Boeing will likely always need partners to help improve worker safety. Sadly, in late 2012, a Boeing painter died from injuries sustained after falling from a scaffold. The company turned to

Zebra Technologies, a maker of physical asset tracking solutions, to develop the Painter Fall Protection Solution. Zebra's ultrawide-band (UWB) radio frequency identification (RFID) sensors are embedded inside the safety harnesses of workers who stand on (and lean over) work platforms called *stackers* that move right, left, up, and down to reach every spot on an airplane's fuselage. Not only does the Painter Fall Protection Solution track the location of workers but it also shuts down the stacker if the worker is not harnessed in properly.

Financial health: This third, and comparatively easy to obtain, situational fit factor concerns finding profitable, free-cash-flow positive prospects who are likely to have open pocketbooks. While most people would be able to name only Boeing and Airbus as airplane manufacturers, there are a decent number of smaller though still sizable competitors to evaluate such as Bombardier, Cessna, Dassault Falcon, and Embraer.

Short term: The fourth situational fit factor arises during executive transitions, especially those of corporate officers or business unit leaders. Case in point: Boeing announced the retirement of CEO W. James McNerney, Jr., on June 22, 2015.[3] His replacement, Dennis A. Muilenburg, as with most executives, will most certainly develop a slew of initiatives to put his own stamp on the company. Similarly, we would be wise to closely monitor changes in senior sales leadership at Salesforce.com. We have found that DiscoverOrg, GainSight, and Relationship Science complement LinkedIn and are excellent sources for detecting changes in leadership. Of course, companies that have great relationships with their clients and prospects know well in advance when such changes are coming.

Value, mission, and culture alignment: The fifth and final set of situational fit factors relate to the "softer side" of target accounts and are the most challenging to ascertain at scale. Here we are

FIGURE 2-2	**Hypothetical Example of Salesforce.com's Original IAP**

FIRMOGRAPHIC	• High-technology companies • Less than 30 employees • Silicon Valley
OPERATIONAL	• No CRM or frustrated with CRM • Preference for expensing versus capitalizing
SITUATIONAL	• Sales leadership transition • Cloud friendly • Socially responsible

talking about whether the prospect is an early or late adopter or has a preference for form versus function. Going back to Boeing, which prides itself on innovation, safety, and diversity, it would be more likely to do business with suppliers sharing the same ethos.

In Figure 2-2, we illustrate a hypothetical example of Salesforce.com's early Ideal Account Profile.

––––––––––

This chapter has covered a litany of firmographic, operational, and situational fit factors. We recommend expending effort only on those factors necessary to allow sales teams to focus on companies with high lifetime value and high likelihood of buying. While institutional knowledge and a modicum of gut feel can often be reliable inputs for selecting factors, a more dependable practice is to examine the shared characteristics of a company's most profitable customers. Compare attributes of your best customers to your worst. If you do not yet have a large customer base, simply interrogate web traffic with an IP lookup service provider like DemandBase or ReachForce to identify which prospects are already interested in your products.

Remember, the Ideal Account Profile (IAP) process identifies the most desirable prospect *companies* to call upon. The next chapter will delve into the Ideal Prospect Persona (IPP) development process so you can accurately target which *individual* decision makers to engage inside those companies.

Crafting Ideal Prospect Personas

The Predictable Prospecting method is all about flooding sales pipelines with the best opportunities in the most efficient way. Even when approaching the ideal segment of companies, sales professionals often fail to engage the right people at the beginning of the process. In this chapter, we will explore the techniques for leveraging an Ideal Prospect Persona (IPP) that will result in higher quality lead generation and greater deal velocity. Moreover, finding and selling to the right person to begin with is *the* most important renewal driver for a recurring revenue business.

Sales (and marketing) professionals often roll their eyes the first time they hear the word *persona* because they think of a persona as an obvious or excessively detailed caricature of a customer. In too many cases, this jaded perception of the word *persona* is correct. And it is precisely for this reason that our persona development approach is designed with the goal of achieving actionable insight that (a) facilitates messaging prospects in the most effective way and (b) ensures a shared understanding across a salesperson's company about the profile of the ideal buyer. Being able to achieve actionable insight on message depends on knowing who the buyers are, what they care about, and how they communicate. Having a shared understanding, for example, is critical for the marketing organization so that it is able to strategically cast its net to catch the right contacts.

In addition, our experience tells us that another major mistake organizations make is defining *too many* personas. While writing this chapter, we engaged a new client with 15 personas! The problem with too many personas is that it violates the rule of having actionable insight that ensures a shared understanding. An organization might target a large number of personas; however, a sales team or individual salesperson cannot and should not be responsible for keeping more than 3 personas in mind. Any more than 3 and persona building becomes another forgotten part of a sales training workshop. While many individuals may be involved in any one buying decision, prospecting personas needs to focus exclusively on those individuals most likely to accept a first meeting. While the ultimate decision maker must be one of the personas, key influencers should also be considered as well as those in a position to provide a warm referral.

Job Title

There is a significant difference between familiar business-to-consumer demographics and the business-to-business demographics that are relevant to our approach. In the B2C world, prospecting personas includes researching personal information such as age, gender, education, marital status, number of dependents in the household, religion, political persuasion, hobbies, household income, and so on. These are precisely the characteristics that induce B2B sales professionals to roll their eyes. While we do not recommend including personal demographics in an Ideal Prospect Persona, since it is used for general targeting, we do support gathering semipersonal information—such as that found on LinkedIn—to help build rapport during specific opportunities. Just be sure to tread lightly when engaging new professional contacts because divulging too much of what you know of their personal background can be off-putting.

A job title is the most commonly leveraged piece of B2B buyer demographic information because it encapsulates both job level and job function. In addition, a job title implies additional information such as specialized knowledge and skills. But there is no benefit in cluttering a persona definition with baseline skills that nearly all individuals in a target population share. The only knowledge and skills worth outlining are those that strongly differentiate the target persona from similar but less attractive professionals. For example, Marylou partners with heads of sales to improve the processes that drive the productivity of their teams. Therefore, she is in a position to assume that a vice president of sales has a strong working knowledge of selling skills, territory management, sales automation tools, and so on. However, it would be in her best interest to segment a population of sales leaders based on their sales development process expertise, especially if that was a deciding factor to enable closing a deal. The problem is that a person's knowledge and skill information are not readily accessible so Marylou needs to discover this during qualification, a topic we explore in Chapter 6.

With respect to job function, it is particularly valuable if you are familiar with the language and the common variations of job titles that prospects use to describe or differentiate themselves. For example, Jeremey engaged heads of learning and development when he worked for the American Management

Association. There he found that this single persona could hold any of the following titles: chief learning officer, vice president of talent development, and director of training, as well as other permutations. Critically, titles included in a persona should align with the data sources used by sales professionals to make finding prospects that much easier.

Professional Objectives

Professional objectives are even more valuable and nearly as common as job titles in persona definitions. Objectives go by many names, including *goals, critical initiatives,* and *key performance indicators* (KPIs). Sales professionals, even beyond the context of their solutions, need to be aware of every major activity that consumes their prospects' time, money, and effort. In addition, a well-defined persona includes the prospect's primary challenges in achieving those objectives, independent of what the salesperson is selling.

Parsing job postings is the most efficient and effective way to develop a holistic picture of the objectives included in an Ideal Prospect Persona. It is important that the jobs chosen to parse are the ones posted by the companies that match the ideal customer profile and are for positions matching the target job title.

Imagine a sales development representative, let's call her Linda, from ValueSelling Associates, one of the top 20 sales training companies,[1] is targeting heads of sales training in the media and entertainment industry. A quick search on LinkedIn reveals a job posting for Spotify, a popular music and video Internet streaming service. Below we have reproduced the company's posting for a head of global ad sales training. Though fairly typical, it is on the long side, even though it doesn't contain the job qualifications or the equal opportunity statement, but bear with us:

> We are looking for an experienced head of training to help develop and run our global sales training function within the Spotify Ad Sales organization. You will be responsible for designing and implementing global and local training programs in order to scale sales training across all our markets, based on the regional teams' needs and market dynamics. These programs will help to educate and develop the sales teams to ensure that business needs are met while improving organizational performance. Your vision and initiatives should align with the overall strategic goals of the company and the ads organization while reflecting our technology, business initiatives, and culture. The result of these short- and long-term efforts should include increased sales, revenue growth, transformation of the business, elevated performance, and an enhanced culture. Above all, your work will affect the way the world experiences music.

What you'll do:
- Understand the different training needs in all markets and partner with sales leaders to define the region and market priorities for sales training and enablement on a quarterly basis
- Design, develop, and deliver effective and innovative training programs that could include onboarding programs and online tutorials, modules, certified training learning assessments, and web-based job aids
- Anticipate needs, resources, time, and budget
- Build relationships with advertising leaders, sales teams, and cross-functional business partners (for example, sales operations, advertising product, marketing teams,

and HR) in the region to collaborate on business needs
and priorities, as well as balancing the training cadence
and sequence based on the overall global priorities and
cadence of the business

- Serve and maintain local external sales training vendors
  for specific training requirements, as needed
- Explore and champion new ideas and experiences to
  improve and enhance training and learning across the
  region and globally
- Leverage global programs to scale training across sales
  teams with consistency and provide iterative feedback,
  while localizing content and training for sales teams'
  needs and market dynamics
- Serve as the project manager for maintaining the design,
  packaging, and delivery of the training experience
- Provide ongoing feedback to the advertising leadership
- Work closely with Spotify's broader learning and development team to build off of and/or integrate any existing
  programs to support the advertising organization
- Work from our office in New York

Obviously a full job description is way too long for an IPP, so
we will isolate, highlight, and focus on the key objectives for this
persona based on success in the role while carefully suppressing
any bias for what we want to sell to them. A well-crafted persona
should fit on a single printed page, which means we must keep
the objectives tightly worded and few in number.

The first and ultimate objective for the head of sales training is to increase sales productivity; if the revenue per associate
for trained individuals does not increase relative to those who
were not trained, then training was clearly a waste of time and
money. As productivity tends to increase as associates become

more tenured, a sales productivity objective should also include a key performance indictor for employee retention—the result of what Spotify refers to as "enhanced culture."

The opportunities the head of sales training will encounter in achieving higher sales productivity can be found in the "What you'll do" section of Spotify's job posting. However, what's missing are two critical pieces that affect average revenue per sales professional and average tenure. These metrics require further refinement to neutralize the impact of hiring (and firing) cycles. Imagine that Spotify's sales professionals have the three levels of maturity fairly typical in B2B sales organizations. First-year associates in learning mode have relatively low productivity. Associates between the first and second years accelerate rapidly. Associates with two years or more have high, stable productivity. In this case, the head of sales training would want to work with her sales operations partner to establish KPIs, one for each of the three tenure ranges. Similarly, rather than overall average tenure, the most relevant KPIs are the retention rates of salespeople tenured less than one year, one to two years, and two or more years. The point to be made here is that an average head of sales training may not recognize the overarching importance of the sales productivity objective or have experience with defining, measuring, and reporting on the KPIs. Linda, our hypothetical sales development representative from ValueSelling Associates, now has the opportunity to move from being "just" another vendor to being a true partner if she can help the head of sales training succeed.

The second objective is to design and deliver high-impact sales training programs. Working within the context of Spotify's job posting, this brief objective statement encapsulates many other factors. The phrase "design and deliver" takes into account global scale with local flair. It also implies that the applicant should have such skills as project management, engaging cross-functional partners to define training priorities, and demonstrating expertise in training tools and techniques. The phrase "high impact" reinforces the contributions to productivity and retention represented in the first objective.

An optional third objective includes managing a network of external sales training partners. Heads of sales training, like all functional leaders, are bombarded on a daily basis by vendors claiming to be the best thing since sliced bread. Since the impact of any particular training program can be assessed only *after* it is experienced, quality is incredibly difficult to assess in advance. Once again, Linda has the opportunity to shift from vendor to partner by doing the unexpected—recommending *other* training providers her clients have successfully used in the past.

Influence Map

The Predictable Prospecting method is focused on securing conversations to initiate and advance the sales cycle. Hence, an Ideal Prospect Persona must include a map of those who influence the decision maker. To illustrate this, consider the visual metaphor of an archery target with three concentric circles (Figure 3-1).

Start by picturing the decision maker sitting alone in the bull's-eye. Corporate buying decisions are complex affairs designed to simultaneously lower risk and ensure support for change. While many people can weigh in with opinions and objections, only one person has the authority to say yes. Working for a large enterprise with over $1 billion in revenue,[2] we can safely assume that the head of sales training at Spotify has the budget and authority to ink contracts with new training partners.

Now picture the direct influencers and gatekeepers that include administrative assistants, corporate attorneys, risk

FIGURE 3-1	Influence Map Bull's-eye

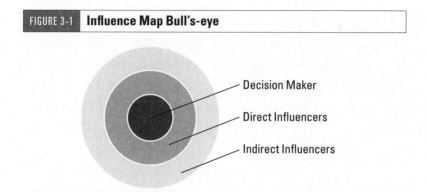

Decision Maker

Direct Influencers

Indirect Influencers

managers, and purchasing agents, among others, sitting in the innermost ring, closest to the bull's-eye. Judging from the Spotify job description, the head of sales training must collaborate with advertising leaders and sales teams, as well as cross-functional partners in human resources, product management, and marketing. Even with decision-making authority, the head of sales training must consult with a combination of people, including her boss (the senior vice president of sales), her subordinates, the head of sales operations, and the chief learning officer.

In the next and outermost ring of the target sit the indirect influencers; these are weaker ties who can be incredibly valuable for generating warm referrals to the decision maker. These indirect influencers may include peers, individual salespeople, and virtually anyone who works for the company. Indirect influencers also exist outside the company in the form of trusted partners or various professional connections. Another important group that belongs in this category of outside influencers consists of the sources the decision maker trusts and turns to for information. A head of sales training will most likely turn to independent sources that include *Selling Power Magazine, Training Industry Magazine*, and the Association for Talent Development.

To complement the influence map, we may go a step further by including critical details about the expected buying process. In addition to the roles likely to be involved in the decision, an Ideal Prospect Persona might also include typical decision-making criteria along with the expected duration of each stage of the sales cycle.

Core Value Proposition and Primary Objections

Up to this point, we have explored Ideal Prospect Persona elements independent of a salesperson's products and services. In articulating the core value proposition and primary objections, we relax the independence constraint.

A great core value proposition should link directly to one or more of the decision maker's major objectives. In addition, because business decisions take time, money, and effort, a great core value proposition must ask, "Why change? Why now? And why with us?" For example, the core value proposition of the Predictable Prospecting model is boosting sales-driving productivity by helping sales professionals secure more meetings with the right people, with less effort.

Assuming the decision maker has the budget and authority, the most common objections Linda might encounter when speaking to the head of sales training at Spotify are the following:

1. *Need:* "Why change?"

   How to overcome: As explained by Chip and Dan Heath in their outstanding book *Switch: How to Change When Change Is Hard*, people accept change when one directs the rider, motivates the elephant, and shapes the path. The rider inside the Spotify training leader's brain is rational and craves testimonials and statistics demonstrating the expected return on learning. The elephant is emotional and must feel she is doing the right thing for the organization. Finally, Linda can shape the path with learning goals, tools, set-back schedules, and so on, making the experience of deploying a globally consistent yet locally tailored training program as effortless as possible.

2. *Trust:* "Why you? I have never heard of you or your company."

   How to overcome: While trust is built by delivering value over time, salespeople trying to secure a meeting do not have that luxury. Hence, social proof in the form of references, case studies of engagements with similar companies, and bylines in well-regarded publications are among the best tools available.

3. *Urgency:* "Why now?"

   How to overcome: While there are many less-than-honest tactics to create a sense of urgency based on scarcity (think "limited time offer while supplies last"), trusted partners create a sense of urgency by linking their products to an organization's strategic objectives. Facing intense competition from Apple, Google, Pandora, and many others, Spotify needs every advantage to enable its sales force to win the most lucrative advertisers.

Personalizing Personas

As mentioned earlier, we recommend keeping business-to-consumer demographics such as education and marital status out of business-to-business Ideal Prospect Personas. By the same token, we also recommend avoiding the common B2C practice of mapping personas to archetypes, a practice popularized by Carol Pearson and Margaret Mark in their 2001 book *The Hero and the Outlaw: Building Extraordinary Brands Through the Power of Archetypes*. This book outlined 12 consumer mindsets: everyman, caregiver, sage, explorer, hero, magician, revolutionary, jester, lover, ruler, creator, and innocent. While knowing these mindsets may help B2C salespeople understand their customers, they are an unnecessary distraction for B2B sales professionals.

The decision on what to include and what to exclude gets a bit murkier when it comes to the professional ambitions of the ideal prospect. The best salespeople help their clients succeed on critical initiatives, the consequences of which may be higher pay, rapid promotion, and greater recognition. In most cases, career goals like these are obvious and they are not directly relevant to selling and servicing clients; therefore, they can be skipped. Related elements found in some B2B personas are day-in-the-life stories (more efficiently expressed by knowledge and skills) and hero stories that paint a picture, like that of a client who buys a product and saves the company.

And now we come to the toughest decision of all—whether or not to personalize a persona with a catchy name and memorable photo. In the plus column, this practice allows a sales organization to share a complex concept in a portable, compact package. We might call the head of sales training "Theresa, the training leader." In the negative column, the practice may turn off sales teams that are more jaded. Since there is no right answer, do what feels right in a given environment.

Information Gathering

Most salespeople and their teams can assemble a fairly complete Ideal Prospect Persona without much extra input. However, we recommend taking time to polish the persona because that investment will pay big dividends during the day-to-day grind of prospecting when having accurate insights concerning prospects can mean the difference between success and failure. Since products and prospects are always in flux, we recommend reviewing and updating personas at least annually.

The first version of an Ideal Prospect Persona needs to be carefully verified by seeking confirming and disconfirming information using a variety of sources. Interviews and surveys of an organization's best customers and hottest prospects are the first places to start, and they can provide the best and most accurate sources of information. Social media, LinkedIn in particular, has become an invaluable source. Additionally, we also turn to external sources such as industry analysts, journalists, complementary vendors who interact with our ideal prospects, and even the prospect's customers.

After refining the Ideal Prospect Persona using insights culled from external sources, one can turn to internal information starting with existing sales and marketing collateral. Anyone who deals with prospects and customers on a regular basis—sales, marketing, customer service, product management, and senior business leaders—is valuable in refining the persona.

In a nutshell, here is the Ideal Prospect Persona we built in this chapter to engage a head of sales training at a media and entertainment company:

- *Decision maker:* Theresa, the training leader

- *Functions:* Head of sales training; sales training director
- Professional objectives
  1. Increase sales productivity and engagement as measured by average revenue per associate (by tenure band) and employee retention rate (by tenure band)
  2. Design and deliver high-impact sales training programs
  3. Manage a network of external sales training partners

- Influence map
  1. *Direct influencers:* Line-of-business leaders and sales leaders, as well as cross-functional partners in human resources, product management, and marketing
  2. *Gatekeepers*: Administrative assistants, corporate counsels, risk managers, and internal finance professionals
  3. *Indirect influencers:* Sales operations peers, talent development peers, and individual sales professionals

- *Our value proposition:* Drive productivity by helping sales professionals secure more meetings with the right people, all with less effort.
  1. *Why change:* Our proven, turnkey, Predictable Prospecting training program can lead to higher productivity and employee retention.
  2. *Why now:* Get the jump on increasingly aggressive competitors.
  3. *Why us:* References and testimonials from elated clients are available on request.

In Part I, we have constructed a Predictable Prospecting targeting model consisting of competitive positioning, an ideal company profile, and an ideal prospect profile. In Part II, we will turn to engaging these targets beginning with crafting messaging that maximizes the odds of securing meetings.

PART II

ENGAGE

Crafting the Right Message

In Part I of this book, we explored *whom* to contact. In Part II, beginning with this chapter, we turn to engaging those right people with the right message (*what*).

Crafting the right message begins with recognizing that prospects exist at different stages of purchase intent in the customer buying cycle as illustrated in Figure 4-1. Effective messaging paves the way for authenticity, starting with initial contact to explore joint values and proceeding through product implementation, delivery, and finally postsale engagement and satisfaction:

FIGURE 4-1   **Stages of the Buying Cycle**

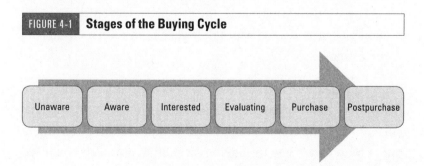

- In the first stage, the prospects are *unaware* of a problem standing in the way of their ability to increase profit, save time, reduce effort, or bolster their reputation. Moreover, at this stage, the prospects are likely oblivious or unconscious of the salesperson's company and products.

- In the second stage, the prospects are *aware* of, yet apathetic to, the problem as well as to the salesperson's company and products.

- In the third stage the prospects are *interested* in and begin to grasp the magnitude of the opportunity and actively seek more detailed information.

- At the end of the fourth stage, the prospects are *evaluating* the magnitude of the opportunity and have a strong, though not yet complete, sense of the vendor's ability to help. Since people are habitual, risk-averse creatures who resist change, the prospects in this stage engage in deliberate rational and emotional consideration, learning more about solutions from various potential partners. The evaluating stage can end with a decision to do nothing, to build, or to buy.

- In the fifth stage, the prospects make a *purchase* and become customers.

- In the sixth and final stage, the prospects seek information *postpurchase* to ensure they get a high return on their investment.

When making initial contact via phone or e-mail, a sales representative must understand and acknowledge the prospects' current level of purchase intent and work to advance that intent one or more stages into the buying cycle. Since prospects contacted during an outbound campaign are typically in the unaware stage, messaging should focus on education directed at the problem rather than on the features of the salesperson's products or the bona fides of her company. One may conjecture that inbound leads are aware, interested, or evaluating. However, all inbound leads are not created equal. While an inbound prospect requesting a demo will at least be interested, another prospect who merely downloaded a white paper on industry best practices may be just as unaware as a random outbound contact. Hence, both content and context matter in crafting messages for Predictable Prospecting.

Finding the Pain

Before we start drafting content for prospects at each stage of the buying cycle, we first need to develop a holistic understanding of the pain they are facing. McKinsey Consulting offers an excellent framework for gaining this insight known as an "issue tree."[1] The first level, or root, of an issue tree poses a question at the highest level of business impact. For instance, a chief marketing officer (CMO) might ask, "How can we increase our return on investment (ROI)?" Most issue tree questions begin with *how*, though *what* and *why* are acceptable as well. These question starters are typically followed by "can" or "does."

As prescribed by McKinsey, each subsequent level of the tree should articulate a mutually exclusive and collectively exhaustive (MECE, pronounced me-see) set of issues—in the form of questions—at the next layer of granularity. *Mutually exclusive* means each of the issues are independent. *Collectively exhaustive* means *every* possible issue is explored at each level. Practically, we work hard to apply the mutually exclusive rule but relax the collectively exhaustive requirement to prevent the issue tree from becoming too unwieldy.

FIGURE 4-2   Issue Tree for a Chief Marketing Officer

In Figure 4-2, the second level of the CMO issue breaks the ROI into its two components, revenue and cost, and the third level breaks those two components down further: revenue is equal to volume times win rate times revenue per transaction; costs can be controlled either by reducing spend on program and people or by increasing productivity.

Issue trees need not be "balanced"; it is just coincidence that the third level lists three items each. In addition, issue trees can, and generally should, go several levels deeper than the one shown in Figure 4-1. But to keep the tree manageable, we can stop expanding it vertically or horizontally whenever the issues are too granular to be of interest to the individual we are attempting to reach. If we were reaching out to a CMO, we would stop expanding early. However, if we were reaching out to a digital marketing manager with the hope of getting a referral to his CMO, then we would expand the tree even more. For example, the question "How can I increase volume?" leads to generating business through direct marketing (postal mail), digital marketing, and phone outreach channels. Digital marketing generates leads via paid traffic from search engine marketing, organic traffic from search engine results, and direct traffic to a website. Organic traffic can be boosted by increasing content volume, content quality, and search engine optimization. And so on . . .

Resources to Validate Prospect Pain

The old adage of measuring twice and cutting once works well here to illustrate our point. Since it is generally agreed that planning is cheap and execution is expensive, taking the time to validate the importance of any given issue is of the utmost importance. This validation step ensures that sales teams not only work the right issues but also express those issues as key in the language of the buyer.

If time permits, interview and survey prospects to validate the pain. In a pinch, the Internet offers countless free tools that provide nearly the same benefits in far less time.

The first set of resources is discussion boards, especially those on LinkedIn Groups and Quora. More broadly, sales professionals should search anywhere they know their prospects and customers congregate, such as blogs and industry and trade websites. Among all of the options, we find Quora especially useful because participants formulate issues in the form of questions that get Upvoted by other readers. Building upon our CMO example, imagine a salesperson focused on selling marketing automation solutions. Entering "marketing automation" in Quora's search yields a link to the topic "Sales and Marketing Automation," which has 8,800 followers. Since it is currently not possible to sort the page by the number of Upvotes, we must scan the page to find the most popular questions. The top five are as follows:

1. Are my marketing automation hopes too high? (64 Upvotes)

2. What is a good online marketing automation tool for B2C startups? (61 Upvotes)

3. What is the best marketing automation tool for small and midsized companies? (60 Upvotes)

4. What are some of the best sales strategies for software-as-a-service (SaaS) products? (47 Upvotes)

5. What is the best marketing automation tool for B2B lead generation? (42 Upvotes)

These five most popular questions are clearly being asked by prospects at later stages—interested or evaluating—of the decision cycle. We find the phrasing of the questions most valuable because it suggests audience segmentation. Notably, business-to-business (B2B) and business-to-consumer (B2C) prospects are in distinct segments as are prospects from small and midsized companies versus those from large enterprises. We also get a sense of two core issues: setting key metrics (from question 1) and lead generation (from question 5).

Outside of the most popular questions, many other key issues appear, including e-mail marketing, lead nurturing, lead scoring, and marketing automation process flows. When scanning the less highly rated questions, salespeople must be very careful to suppress the tendency to focus on only those topics of most interest to them. To overcome this phenomenon, known as *confirmation bias*, we recommend cataloging the questions in descending order by the total number of Upvotes each collected. That way you can rule out more esoteric questions such as, "What are some tools similar to Yozio?" (which was posed as veiled self-promotion by one of its cofounders, albeit with full disclosure) and rule in such questions as, "What are the key challenges in marketing automation?"

The second set of resources involves language. These are the words that marketers use to leverage the generation of the keywords used in search engine optimization (SEO) and search engine marketing (SEM). There are two subsets of tools: the first suggests keywords using a website URL as input, and the second suggests more specific keywords using less specific keywords as input.

The Google Adwords Keyword Planner is a great starting point since it is a hybrid of both subsets and relies on an incredibly sophisticated algorithm. In its current incarnation, we entered "marketing automation" for "Your product or service," "www.marketo.com" (a pure-play marketing automation vendor) for "Your landing page," and "sales and marketing software" for "Your product category." In ranking the keyword ideas generated from highest to lowest, and based on average monthly searches, the issues that bubble to the top include CRM software, e-mail marketing, demand generation, lead management, lead generation, lead nurturing, sales tools, lead scoring, and so on. As expected, these reinforce the topics we discovered on Quora.

Get a second opinion by using one of the countless Internet options by simply searching "keyword generator" (without quotation marks). Our favorite sites are Ranksonic.com, Keywordtool.io, and ubersuggest.org. We even built one of our own, which you can check out at keyword-oracle.com. In contrast to Google's Keyword Planner, these tools are narrower in scope, allowing users to view suggestions after entering *either* a URL *or* a phrase.

The Compel with Content (CWC) Story Framework

The effective crafting of any content is highly context- and time-dependent. Though we are about to share best practices, frameworks, and a number of real examples, we encourage you to craft your own original content using our templates as starting points. With this caveat, let's get started with the Compel with Content (CWC) framework developed by Marylou Tyler.[2]

The CWC framework applies classic storytelling techniques to Predictable Prospecting communications. As with any writing exercise, the CWC framework begins with planning. Our favorite planning method involves thoughtfully filling in the following blanks:

For whom? _____

To do what? _____

In order to? _____

By what means? _____

To illustrate, let's pick the "How can I increase volume?" question from the issue tree in Figure 4-2. Our response is in Figure 4-3.

FIGURE 4-3   **A Response to the "How Can I Increase Volume?" Question Posed in Figure 4-2**

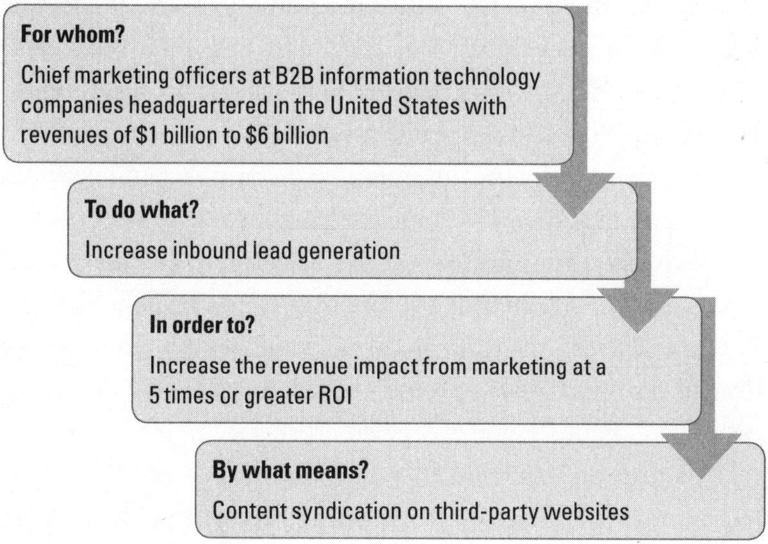

For whom?
Chief marketing officers at B2B information technology companies headquartered in the United States with revenues of $1 billion to $6 billion

To do what?
Increase inbound lead generation

In order to?
Increase the revenue impact from marketing at a 5 times or greater ROI

By what means?
Content syndication on third-party websites

The Trigger

Next, you must decide on the *trigger* (or tone) of the message you want to convey because the buying stage determines whether the trigger should be emotional or rational. Keep in mind that messages designed to move prospects from unaware to aware and from aware to interested are primarily if not wholly emotional. Messages designed to move prospects from interested to evaluating and from evaluating to purchase are predominantly rational.

The Three Os

As with many story frameworks, CWC relies upon a three-act structure with the handy mnemonic of three Os: obstacle, outcome, and opportunity.

Obstacle presents a *single* problem and/or challenge from the prospect's perspective. Often, one can leap right into the problem;

other times, a sentence or two is necessary to provide situational context.

Outcome presents the solution. Dramatic examples of how a salesperson has helped other customers turn their businesses around, particularly those similar to the target prospect, represent better solutions than product benefits.

Opportunity refocuses attention on the prospect and provides a *single* call to action. We emphasize *single* because sales professionals often cram multiple calls to action into a single e-mail or voice mail. As we will explore deeply in the next chapter, Predictable Prospecting involves many touches, providing ample time to try out different problem-solution sets and a variety of calls to action in front of any given prospect.

In an example of how this all comes together, the following e-mail was designed specifically to move a prospect from unaware to aware:

Subject: Inbound Lead Generation Survey Findings

Hi <Prospect_First_Name>,

We recently surveyed 500 CMOs at information technology companies about their marketing strategies, and I thought you'd like to see the results.

The survey reveals that the number one priority for marketing leaders is increasing the number of inbound leads. However, only 10 percent of those same leaders felt their programs were highly successful.

You can download the report now to discover the best practices of companies with winning inbound lead generation programs.

Warm regards,

<Rep_First_Name>

From Unaware to Aware

One of the biggest mistakes sales professionals make is assuming that prospects are ready to buy from the moment of first contact. These beliefs are reinforced by selective memories of one-and-done deals and by admonitions to "always be closing." Over the course of several days, we saved and analyzed 281 unsolicited sales and marketing e-mails. Among those, 43 percent asked for a meeting! Although it is possible for individuals to skip buying-cycle stages, we recommend crafting Predictable Prospecting messaging with the goal of moving forward one stage at a time. To that end, we begin by crafting content designed to move a prospect from unaware to aware. This process, especially if it contains great messaging, increases the prospects' awareness of the problem and their trust in the ability of a company and salesperson to provide a low-risk, high-return solution.

During outbound campaigns, the salesperson should start with the expectation that prospects are unaware or unappreciative of the problem or of the salesperson's ability to solve it. When prospects are unaware, it is too soon to ask for a meeting. Instead, the relationship should be initiated by the salesperson by sharing resources that are brief, high value, educational, and product-agnostic such as blog posts, infographics, and video clips.

Personalizing Communication

There are three degrees of personalization:

- Fully generic

- Mass-personalized

- Hyperpersonalized

The salesperson must rely on experience and intuition to accurately gauge the degree of personalization to apply. The more personalized the communication, the higher the likelihood of a response. It's true that personalized communications take time to research and write, but with plenty of inexpensive and sophisticated e-mail marketing tools available, mass-personalized communications easily eliminate the need to ever deploy fully generic messages.

In the earlier stages of the buying cycle, particularly in the unaware stage, mass-personalized communications will almost always be optimal. The exception to this rule is when a salesperson is targeting a very limited number of accounts in the unaware stage. In this case, *every* communication must be hyperpersonalized. Regardless of territory strategy, the level of personalization must increase during the later stages of the buying cycle.

So, what does a decent mass-personalized e-mail to an unaware prospect look like? Here is a good example:

From: <rep_e-mail_address>

Subject: Mobile Optimization Renaissance

Hi <Prospect_First_Name>,

I thought you'd find this article on mobile optimization helpful—about 50 percent of consumers say they won't return to a website if it doesn't load properly on their mobile device, meaning nearly half of potential customers could be turned away if a website isn't optimized correctly.

<Blog_Post_URL>

If you'd like to learn more about our approach to optimizing and creating breakthrough mobile experiences, I'd love to set up a short call. Are you available anytime in the upcoming weeks? Or, if you don't oversee the digital agency

(continued)

selection process, would you please refer me to the best contact?

Thank you,

<Rep_First_Name> <Rep_Last_Name>
<Rep_Phone_Number>
<Rep_Company_URL>

*<Rep_Company_Name> is a digital agency that lives at the intersection of marketing and technology. We design and develop award-winning mobile solutions for clients such as FreshDirect, IDT, and Hewlett-Packard.

This e-mail demonstrates many best practices for engaging prospects in the unaware stage. We appreciate that the e-mail appears to have been sent by a real person: it has a nongeneric sender address, it is written in simple text without images, and it has a normal signature. Of the 281 unsolicited sales and marketing e-mails we received, 66 percent came from what appeared to be a real person's e-mail address. The other one-third were the equivalent of presorted postal mail and faced the same fate of being sent straight to trash without a moment's consideration.

We also appreciated that the e-mail was written the way normal people format their e-mails, in simple text. Of the 281 e-mails, 35 percent used simple text, 25 percent used enhanced text (distinguished from simple text by the use of bold, italics, color, or highlighting), and 40 percent used image-heavy formatting.

MailChimp, a popular e-mail marketing service provider, analyzed 40 million e-mails sent via their platform and concluded, "This might sound dead simple, but here you have it: your subject line should (drum roll please) describe the subject of your e-mail. Yep, that's it. . . . When it comes to e-mail marketing, the best subject lines tell what's inside, and the worst subject lines sell what's inside."[3] We agree.

ReturnPath, an e-mail optimization and fraud protection provider, analyzed subject lines and the resulting read rates of e-mails received by over 2 million subscribers from over 3,000 senders.[4] Here are ReturnPath's most valuable key findings relevant to Predictable Prospecting:

- Urgency is king.

    "Subject lines that convey a sense of urgency were the top performers." Effective keywords include "still time," "limited time," and "expiring." Though ReturnPath did not comment on the word "urgent," other studies confirmed it works well too.

- Subject line length does not matter!

    While the majority of e-mails have subject lines between 41 and 50 characters, there was no correlation between subject line length and read rate. The only noticeably bad length is anything over 100 characters. In our 281-e-mail sample, the average subject line length was 44 characters, and only 3 percent were over 100 characters—the longest of which, 115 characters, read as follows: "<Live Webinar> Must Sees at Dreamforce: The Latest Sales Effectiveness Insights and Trends from Smart Selling Tools."

- Prospects want new, fast, elegant, and easy but not cheap solutions.

    The keywords "new," "fastest," "prettiest," and "easiest" had a positive influence on read rates. However, almost every word describing price had a negative impact, including

"cheapest," "clearance," "sale," percent," "$," and "free."
As an unusual and unexplainable aside, "fastest" works,
but "quickest" does not.

- Prospects can smell clickbait from a mile away.

  The provocative subject line "Shocking secrets you won't
  believe" is about as ineffective as it gets because the words
  "shocking," "secret," and "won't believe" all perform well
  below average. The only phrase of this ilk that works moderately well is "what you need to know," probably because
  it hints at education.

- Call-to-action words are effective.

  Imperative words, such as "register," "open," and, to a lesser
  extent, "download," have a positive influence on read rates,
  but "buy" and "call" have a negative impact and should be
  avoided.

- Nobody wants to read about you or your news.

  "Announcing," "introducing," "learn," "read," and "see" all
  perform poorly since they ask recipients to expend effort
  with little implied benefit, as do the personal pronouns
  "I," "me," my," and "our." By the same token, please do not
  send out press releases, which, fortunately, accounted for
  only 1 percent of the e-mails we analyzed.

- Convey concrete, immediately actionable recommendations.

  "Steps" and "ways" work better than "how to" and "why."

ReturnPath's findings are consistent with an earlier study
by MailChimp analyzing approximately 24 billion (yes, billion)

delivered e-mails.[5] In addition to the findings above, MailChimp's study also revealed the following:

- Subject line name personalization, particularly using both first *and* last names, is highly effective. (*Note:* In our study of 281 e-mails, 89 percent had no subject line personalization, 5 percent included only one of our company names, 5 percent included only the first name for one of us, and 1 percent included *both* of our first names *and* both company names. None included both first and last names, suggesting this practice may have gone out of vogue. Another study by MailerMailer,[6] however, found subject line personalization to be highly ineffective, so test carefully and proceed with caution.)

- "Thank you" is highly effective, but this may be because the phrase is common in confirmation e-mails and therefore not appropriate for a first-touch e-mail.

- Capitalizing the first letter of every word is better than capitalizing only the first letter of the first word. (Exclamation marks and ALL CAPS should be avoided at all times.)

- "Sign up" is not effective. It implies effort with uncertain reward.

- Subject lines that pose questions perform well.[7]

As with everything in the Predictable Prospecting process, "Always be testing," because response rates are contextually dependent on the buying stage, vendor, product, prospect demographics, and so on. For instance, MailChimp found that first-name personalization in the subject line was highly effective for government recipients, but it was highly ineffective for legal industry recipients. In addition, ReturnPath found "last chance" had a positive effect while MailChimp found that same phrase had a negative effect. Making matters even more complicated, techniques rise and fall in effectiveness as they cycle through periods of under- and overuse.

Let's get back to our sample e-mail. First off, we appreciated the personalized salutation, even if it was computer generated. In our sample, 59 percent of e-mails used the recipient's first name.

The body of the e-mail is also well crafted. Rather than starting with the overused and ineffective "My name is <rep_first_name> from <rep_company>," the text opens with value by offering exactly what we prescribe—a short, educational, and product-agnostic resource. The text immediately establishes the problem: "Nearly half of potential customers could be turned away if a website isn't optimized correctly."

E-mails to unaware prospects can certainly end without any call to action other than the link to the free resource. A good marketing automation platform will capture the click, migrate the prospect to the next stage in the campaign, and alert the salesperson; the click is a *signpost* that signals advancement to the next stage in the buying cycle. This e-mail even goes a few steps further in the event the prospect is already more advanced in the buying cycle. The final body paragraph applies the ubiquitous tactic of asking for a short call or a referral to a person who would benefit from solving the problem. Additionally, the post-script after the salesperson's signature introduces the company and provides links to case studies without cluttering the body of the e-mail. These extras are not inherently good or bad; they should be A/B tested to determine their effectiveness.

Let's turn briefly to hyperpersonalized messaging for unaware prospects. In broad brushstrokes, the e-mail should read as follows:

From: <rep_e-mail_address>

Subject: <Hyperpersonalized_Subject_Line>

<Prospect_First_Name>,

I noticed <relevant_professional_or_business_finding_from_precadence_research>.

The reason for my e-mail is that I'd like to share how we partnered with <company_similar_to_prospect's_organization> to achieve <results_relevant_to_prospect>.

Do you have time for a quick call to explore whether or not we might be a fit for <accelerating_a_specific_prospect_initiative_or_solving_a_specific_prospect_problem>?

Please advise,

<Rep_First_Name>
<Rep_First_Name> <Rep_Last_Name>
<Rep_Phone_Number>
<Rep_Company_URL>

From Aware to Interested

During a prospect's journey from aware to interested, she is willing to invest more time getting educated about the problem and any potential solutions. To meet her needs, the salesperson should serve up more detailed content, including reports on topics, trends, and best practices; product-agnostic webinars; information-rich landing pages; and diagnostic tools. Reports and webinars are well established so we need not expand on them here. Information-rich landing pages provide insights on trends and best practices. Diagnostic tools are a relatively new phenomenon, and the best ones offer compelling value to the prospect and are virtually free of cost to the vendor. HubSpot's Marketing Grader[8] is a frequently cited example, and it scans a website and then provides a prescriptive report on the site's digital marketing effectiveness complete with actionable recommendations. Many companies are putting their high-value tools online to enhance lead generation.

The following is a good example of a mass-personalized e-mail designed to move a prospect from the aware stage to the interested stage:

From: <rep_e-mail_address>

Subject: Simplified Analytics

Dear <Prospect_First_Name>,

I thought you would find this Gartner Market Guide valuable as the quarter is still at an early start.

Predictability for the Sales Executive: Simplifying Machine Learning Analytics for Sales & Marketing

Expectations for growth and revenue have never been higher for sales teams than they are today. Fortunately, the technology we now have available is making it possible for companies to have a predictable pipeline. <Company_Name> is revolutionizing the sales process by making the forecast more reliable, enriching data in the CRM, and applying smart analytics to define, align, and evolve.

Find out how you can start closing 90 percent of your forecasted deals here.

Thanks,

<Rep_First_Name> <Rep_Last_Name>
<Rep_Title>

This example has much in common with the unaware to aware e-mail. It delivers value immediately in the form of a research report from Gartner, a respected, independent, objective third party. Next, the body states the problem: "Expectations for growth and revenue have never been higher for sales teams than they are today." With the problem established, the text shares that solutions are available: "Fortunately, the technology we now have available is making it possible for companies to have a predictable pipeline." After setting up the problem and suggesting that various solutions are available, the e-mail has earned the right to highlight the company and the value proposition of its products: "<Company_Name> is revolutionizing the sales process by making the forecast more reliable, enriching data in the CRM, and applying smart analytics to define, align, and evolve." Though the line "Find out how you can start closing 90 percent of your forecasted deals here" is unnecessary content-wise, it is considered a best practice to include links three times: once at the beginning, once in the middle, and once at the end.

To recap: Provide value, set up the problem, suggest the existence of multiple solutions, present the company and/or product and its high-level value proposition, and embed a single (although it's fine if it is repeated) call to action. In all, the body of this e-mail is a mere 104 words. By comparison the average body length of the 281 e-mails we studied was 253, or more than double that.

From Interested to Evaluating

Once a prospect is interested, the salesperson has the opportunity to provide an array of resources proving the company's differentiated ability to solve the problem. Effective assets designed to move a prospect from interested to evaluating include case studies, testimonials, product reviews, product-centric webinars, on-demand demonstration videos, comparison charts, and discovery meetings.

While messaging at this point should often become more customized, mass-personalization is sufficient if the salesperson has a large number of prospects. Here is an example of a mass-personalized e-mail we received that encouraged us to register for a product-centric webinar:

From: <rep_e-mail_address>

Subject: Exclusive Invitation for <Prospect_Company_Name>

Hi <Prospect_First_Name>,

On behalf of <Rep_Company>, I would personally like to invite you to an exclusive preview we are hosting on <u>Event Date and Time></u>, where our <Executive_Title>, <Executive_Name> will be giving a tour of <u><Company's Product></u>.

This <short_product_description> is being released on <Release_Date>, and we are pleased to offer you a first peek at this new and exciting subscription-based service.

Please join us to see firsthand how <Company's_Product> empowers you to enhance your market research and deliver tangible results by:

- <Benefit_1>
- <Benefit_2>
- <Benefit_3>

Please reserve your spot at: <Registration_Page_URL>.

(Please note: Space is limited. Deadline to sign up is <RSVP_Date>.)

If you're not able to attend on this date, please reach out to me directly, and we can arrange a personal demonstration.

Sincerely,

<Rep_First_Name> <Rep_Last_Name>
<Rep_Title>, <Rep_Company>
<Rep_Phone>

This e-mail applies many of the best practices we have already discussed concerning the sender address, the subject, and the body. However, the call to action appropriately shifts from product-agnostic to product-specific. The bulleted list reinforces and adds to the prospect's understanding of the company's ROI-driven value proposition. The last sentence engages prospects who prefer a personal touch, "If you're not able to attend on this date, please reach out to me directly, and we can arrange a personal demonstration." Asking for a discovery meeting is appropriate when moving from interested to evaluating, and this offer of a one-on-one product demonstration conveys a gentle means to that end.

From Evaluating to Purchase

Since this is a chapter on messaging in a book about prospecting, we will touch only briefly on communications designed to move a prospect from evaluating to purchase. As one might expect, e-mails and voice mails in this stage must be completely personalized and must offer superior value in the form of trials (free or paid), consultative diagnostics, ROI calculators, references, and, ultimately, proposals. Many of these assets are scarce, expensive, time-consuming, or all three. Hence, they should be leveraged only when a salesperson has a reasonably high degree of confidence that a prospect is near purchase.

The following e-mail is from a sales executive who completed a consultative analysis, an audit of inbound sales response effectiveness, for one of the authors:

From: <rep_e-mail_address>

Subject: Results of Interviews/<Prospect_Company_Name> Sales Process

Hi <Prospect_First_Name>,

As we talked about in our conversation a couple of weeks ago, I've reviewed the "response audit" we provided, and I have taken it a couple of steps further.

I took information gathered from you and your team, and we've come up with some recommendations and a couple of case studies (see attached).

A couple of points:

- Each rep is spending at least 40 minutes per day leaving voice mails (7,280 hours per year for the team). We can help you get much of that time back.

- Inbound calling time is not measured or monitored, and that seems to be where a lot of sales value-added is occurring (or being lost). We can help you track, measure, and tune inbound activities.

- We can minimize inter-team conflicts (different teams going after the same business); we can help draw clear lines within the Salesforce.com environment.

- Sixty dials is a great metric. Ten percent contact rate isn't. We can help you increase that contact rate.

Take a look at the document, and let me know your thoughts. Based on what we've learned, I'd like to talk further about the possibility of implementing <Rep_Product> concurrently with Salesforce. I believe we can present a strong business case.

Sincerely,

<Rep_First_Name> <Rep_Last_Name>
<Rep_Title>
<Rep_Phone>

While the sales representative who crafted the above e-mail started with a template, the e-mail is hyperpersonalized and offers tremendous value in the body and in the attachments (not shown).

Table 4-1 summarizes the Compel with Content (CWC) strategy by buying cycle stage.

TABLE 4-1	**The Compel with Content (CWC) Strategy by Buying Cycle Stage**			
BUYING STAGE →	**UNAWARE TO AWARE**	**AWARE TO INTERESTED**	**INTERESTED TO EVALUATING**	**EVALUATING TO PURCHASE**
Industry and Role Problem Focus	High focus, low detail	High focus, medium detail	High focus, high detail	Low focus, low detail
Prospect-Specific Problem Focus	None	None	Low	High
Vendor and Product Focus	None	Low	Medium	High
Personalization	Mass-personalized	Mass-personalized with data-driven intelligence derived from previous interactions	Mass-personalized or lightly customized	Hyperpersonalized
Triggers	High emotional; low rational	High emotional; medium rational	Medium emotional; medium rational	Low emotional; high rational
Prospect Time Commitment with Content	< 10 seconds	< 5 minutes	< 20 minutes	< 60 minutes
Content	• Blog post • Infographic • Short video	• Report or white paper • E-book • Diagnostic tool • Webinar	• Case study • Testimonial • Product review • Comparison chart • Discovery meeting	• Trial (free or paid) • ROI calculator • Reference • Consultative analysis • Proposal

Getting Meetings Through Prospecting Campaigns

Now that you have a high-level understanding of how to craft compelling content, it's time to explore the right channels and the right frequencies for delivering messages in ways proven to secure meetings that ultimately win business.

To frame this properly, we need to take a moment to explore the life cycle of a lead as illustrated in Figure 5-1.

Prospects enter the sales cycle with their lead status set to *New*. Alternative labels for this status include *Cold*, *Marketing Qualified Lead* (MQL), *Not Attempted*, and *Open*. A new lead may come from an inbound source such as a white paper download or from an outbound source such as a rented list.

After receiving a new lead, the salesperson must decide whether to accept or reject it. Leads are primarily rejected for one of the following three reasons. First, the data may be too corrupt to clean, in which case it should be soft deleted from

FIGURE 5-1 | **Predictable Prospecting Lead Life Cycle**

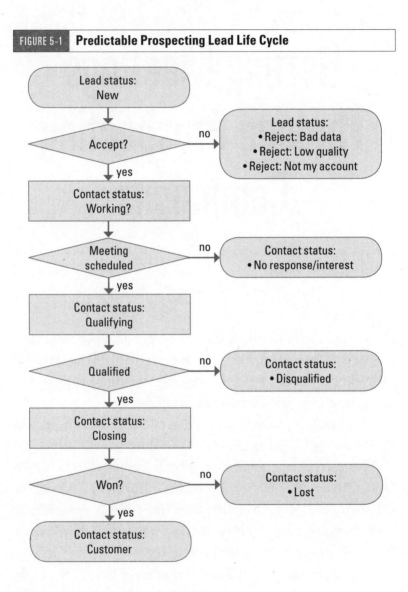

both the marketing automation platform (MAP) and the customer relationship management (CRM) system. Second, the salesperson may judge the lead to be low quality for a variety of reasons, including but not limited to poor firmographic fit, poor demographic fit, or a prior negative experience with the prospects or their company. Third, the salesperson can flag as "Not my account" if the lead was incorrectly assigned, triggering manual reassignment by sales operations.

Once a salesperson does accept a lead, it advances into the *Working* contact status. Some sales organizations refer to this status as *Attempting, Contacting,* or *sales accepted lead* (SAL), and we will concentrate the bulk of this chapter on this contact status since advancement to the next stage depends upon securing this first meeting. If the salesperson is unable to secure a meeting either because the prospect was unresponsive or was unambiguously uninterested, then the contact status should be set to *No response or interest* so the prospect can be returned to automated nurturing after a cooling off period.

Critically, the Predictable Prospecting system recommends holding prospects in the Leads category for as short a time as possible, which is why accepted New *leads* advance to Working *contacts.* By way of reminder, most CRM systems treat leads as independent entities. Leads convert to contacts when associated with a new or existing account. In addition, the account (and selected contacts) may be linked to a new or existing opportunity. We strongly prefer working prospects as contacts rather than as leads in order to have a persistent picture of inbound and outbound prospect activities for a holistic view of what is happening in each account.

After that most important first meeting is secured, the prospect advances to *Qualifying* contact status, sometimes labeled *Converting.* (The next chapter covers this richly detailed and highly nuanced stage.) If the prospect fails to meet qualifying criteria, the salesperson sets the account status to *Disqualified* so the prospect may return to automated nurturing.

Once a lead is qualified, it converts to the *Closing* contact status. If all goes well, a prospect advances to the final contact status, *Customer*, commonly labeled as *Client, Transacted or Won*, or simply *Won*. Alternatively, if the prospect does not purchase, the account status is set to *Lost* and returned to automated nurturing.

When to Add Granularity to the Sales Cycle

Much to the dismay of salespeople who justifiably dread busy-work, sales leaders are constantly tempted to increase the granularity of each Lead Status and Contact Status category. For instance, No Response or Interest could be split into No Response and a multitude of reasons for No Interest. Similarly, Disqualified could be broken down into reasons associated with qualification criteria; for those organizations using the ubiquitous BANT approach, one would have Disqualified—budget, Disqualified—authority, Disqualified—need, and Disqualified—timing.

There is no absolute right or wrong level or granularity; there is only right or wrong for a given sales organization. However, we do offer the following guidance: the right reason to add a lead or contact status item is if the new item is crucial for optimizing pipeline velocity and success. For instance, if prospects begin to pile up in the New Queue, then marketing may need to increase its scoring threshold to provide fewer higher-quality leads. Or if prospects get stuck in the Qualifying Queue, then the qualification process likely needs evaluation and additional structure.

Avoid adding granularity when doing so only enhances reporting. For example, it may not matter from a sales process optimization perspective whether contacts were not responsive versus not interested in which case the deeper reporting is not worth the added sales complexity. When in doubt, choose simplicity. You can always add complexity later as you begin to understand your unique situation.

Building the New Queue

The top of the sales funnel starts with a robust volume of prospects in the New lead status queue who, importantly, match the ideal prospect profile. At a high level, there are two groups of lead sources: inbound and outbound.

Inbound leads are generally the most desirable since they indicate some degree of recent exposure to the salesperson's company or products or some degree of recently expressed interest in solving a problem addressed by the salesperson's company. Most inbound leads come from digital and traditional marketing programs, including digital content marketing (webinars, white papers, blog subscriptions, and so on), trade show badge scans, and events.

Response time for online leads is particularly critical as proven by an oft-cited study jointly conducted by MIT and InsideSales.com.[1] The researchers found the odds of contacting a lead are 100 times higher in the first 5 minutes compared to the first 30 minutes and 10 times higher in the first hour compared to all longer durations combined; the odds of reaching a prospect exhibit rapid exponential decay. Even more importantly, the odds of qualifying a lead, which the researchers defined as having a meaningful conversation with a key decision maker, are 21 times higher in the first 5 minutes compared to the first 30 minutes and 6 times higher in the first hour compared to all longer durations combined. These results make intuitive sense since prospects are likely to be both available and interested just after submitting their information.

Outbound leads can be broken down into three types, two of which we recommend. The best starts with an organization's house list. Usually, the most valuable prospects on a house list are former clients, followed by prospects lost after qualification, followed by prospects who were disqualified, followed by prospects who were not interested or did not reply to prior attempts to set a discovery meeting. In addition, many sales and marketing organizations supplement their house list by gathering ideal prospects from high-quality sources such as LinkedIn.

The next best type is rented lists. Among rented lists, the best ones for B2B are supplied by trade publications since prospects are fresher and have opted in. In the case of e-mail-only (or direct-mail-only) lists, the owner deploys a campaign on the renter's behalf not only reducing effort but also protecting the e-mail reputation of the renter. (Mass e-mailing is fraught with risk because senders can be flagged as spammers, which will affect the delivery of *any* type of e-mail. In addition, it is easy to run afoul of various anti-spam laws, leading to significant fines.)

When renting a list, we recommend piloting with a small sample to determine the expected return on investment (ROI). For example, imagine a company has a 5 times the ROI threshold; that is, the profit from the list rental needs to exceed the cost by 5 times. Currently, e-mail lists range from $0.10 to $0.50 per name per mailing. So, imagine you send 100,000 e-mails consisting of a content marketing offer linked to a landing page at a cost of $250 per thousand (in industry parlance, a "250 CPM"), equal to $25,000 of the total cost. Using a typical average[2] open rate of 20 percent and a typical average click-through rate

(CTR) of 3 percent nets 600 prospects who arrive at the landing page.

Conversion rates, measured as visitors who complete a registration form, vary widely, but we will use 30 percent because rates from e-mail exceed rates from paid search engine clicks. Hence, we are down to 180 leads at a cost of $139 per lead. Now, we can calculate the win rate needed to achieve 5 times ROI based on the customer lifetime value. For instance, if the customer's lifetime value is $50,000, then the win rate would need to be 1.6 percent, or 3 wins out of the 180 leads (Table 5-1).[3]

TABLE 5-1	E-mail Marketing Return-on-Investment Calculation

(1)	Enter cost per thousand contact records:	$250
(2)	Enter number of contacts:	100,000
(3)	Multiply (1) by (2), and divide by 1,000 to get the total cost:	$25,000
(4)	Enter the expected open rate:	20%
(5)	Multiply (2) by (4) to get the total number of opens:	20,000
(6)	Enter the expected click-through rate:	3%
(7)	Multiply (5) by (6) to get the number of landing page visitors:	600
(8)	Enter the landing page conversion rate:	30%
(9)	Multiply (7) by (8) to get the number of leads:	180
(10)	Enter the expected win rate:	1.66%
(11)	Multiply (9) by (10) to get the number of wins:	3
(12)	Enter the lifetime value per win:	$50,000
(13)	Multiply (11) by (12) to get the expected revenue:	$150,000
(14)	Calculate [(13) − (3)]/(13) to get the ROI:	5.0

There are many reputable, and many more disreputable, e-mail list sellers and renters. In addition to the previously mentioned trade publications, some reputable vendors our clients have used include Discover.org, Data.com, Dun & Bradstreet (which owns

NetProspex), InfoUSA, and ZoomInfo. For do-it-yourselfers, there is an excellent mailing list finder available from NextMark at http://lists.nextmark.com/. For those willing to outsource, a practice we recommend, there is a cottage industry of list brokers available to help; one we have used with success, Merit Direct, is one of the larger ones.

The third type, and one which we do not recommend, is purchased lists. If a provider is willing to sell a list, the list has almost certainly been spammed beyond recognition, collected through illicit or unethical means, or filled with out-of-date records.

Regardless of source, all lists must be judiciously cleaned before distributing contacts to salespeople. In our experience, the three most important fields to append and verify are e-mail address, phone number, and LinkedIn profile URL. With respect to phone number, strive to acquire the direct dial. If you cannot obtain the direct dial, then try to find a number to access the company's dial-by-name directory; access the dial-by-name directory from voice mail using the key combinations shown in Table 5-2. Worst case, you will need to dial the company's main number. If you end up in this last situation, be prepared to develop a friendship with the switchboard operator.

TABLE 5-2	Dial-by-Name Directory Access
TELEPHONE SYSTEM	**DIAL-BY-NAME DIRECTORY ACCESS**
Audix	*8, then either **6 or *2
Avaya	*8
Cisco	*, then #, then 4
Inter-tel	*, then 1
Meridian	*70 or *7#
Octel	* (or 0)
Siemens	* (or 0)

Building a New Queue as a Continual Process

Finally, we need to stress that building the New Queue is a continual process. Some prospects engage, some are unresponsive, some opt out, and some leave a company or are no longer in a role matching the Ideal Prospect Persona. Leads must be replenished to minimum watermark levels to prevent the pipeline from running dry.

A sample list replenish waterfall looks like this for every 100 records:

- 3 prospects are actively looking for a solution.

- 7 are open to hearing about what you have to offer.

- 30 know they do not want your product.

- 30 aren't sure how relevant your product is for them.

- 30 don't know they need what you have.

Given these numbers, it is likely that after one full prospecting cycle, approximately 40 percent (3 percent actives plus 7 percent maybes plus 30 percent don't want it) of your initial list needs to be replaced for the next prospecting cycle.

Building a Customer Referral Program

As a New Queue lead source, referred leads are distinct from inbound and outbound leads. Referral programs generate higher win rates, faster deal velocity, and higher lifetime value. In addition, customers who provide referrals are likely to have higher retention rates, even when compared to other customers with the same satisfaction, due to the psychological principle of consistency.

Referrals work because people trust people, especially people like themselves, more than they trust any other source of information, as shown in Table 5-3.[4] This survey by Nielsen polled more than 29,000 people in 58 countries.

TABLE 5-3	**Trust in Advertising**

FORM OF ADVERTISING	PERCENTAGE WHO COMPLETELY OR SOMEWHAT TRUST
Recommendations from people I know	84
Branded websites	69
Consumer opinions posted online	68
Ads on TV	62
Ads served in search engine results	48
Online banner ads	42

Source: Nielsen, "Global Trust in Advertising and Brand Messages," September 2013, http://www.nielsen.com/content/dam/corporate/us/en/reports-downloads/2013%20Reports/Nielsen-Global-Trust-in-Advertising-Report-September-2013.pdf.

Referral program success is not only a business-to-consumer phenomenon. A study of hundreds of business-to-business companies (see Figure 5-2) found that referred leads close at more than twice the rate of any other source.[5] Though the overall average lead-to-deal conversion rate of 0.8 percent may seem low, the results are consistent with our experience. According to the study by Implisit, 13 percent of leads convert to opportunity after an average time to conversion of 84 days. Then, 6 percent of opportunities progress to a closed deal after an average time to win of 18 days.

One of our favorite turns of phrase describing the most important factor of a successful referral program is "Be referable." When a company delights its customers with exceptional product

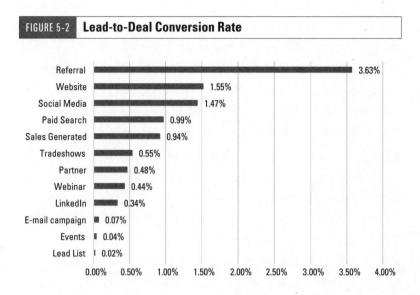

| FIGURE 5-2 | **Lead-to-Deal Conversion Rate** |

Source: Implisit, https://www.implisit.com/blog/b2b-sales-benchmarks/.

and service experiences, customers are delighted to provide referrals as a gift to their friends and colleagues.

In nearly all cases, one must deliver value before asking for a referral. The timing of the ask should be guided by the peak-end rule,[6] which relies on evidence that people judge an experience based on how pleasant (or unpleasant) it is at its peak and at its end. Consequently, our best advice is to conduct a Net Promoter Score (NPS) survey either at the expected peak or, more practically, at the end of a service experience. An NPS survey asks the simple question, "On a scale of 0 to 10, 10 highest, how likely are you to recommend _____ to a friend or a colleague?" According to its trademark owners (Fred Reichheld, Bain & Company, and Satmetrix), promoters give ratings of 9 or 10, passives give ratings of 7 or 8, and detractors give ratings of 6 or lower. It is a no-brainer to ask for a recommendation after receiving a rating of 9 or 10, though shockingly few companies actually close this loop. (Since all rules are meant to be broken, the exception to the ask-after-service rule is when the value of a service is enhanced by having friends and colleagues be part of the experience, as is the case in social networks and live events. In those instances, go for the referral when onboarding the new client.) Similarly, one must go into service recovery mode for the strongest detractors, particularly those with ratings of 0 to 2.

In addition to driving growth via referrals and retention via service recovery, sending NPS surveys at a regular cadence helps identify when customers move on. This is valuable because it is much easier to win recent B2B customers back soon after they switch jobs than it is to win a prospect who is less familiar with us. Tracking B2B movement remains a manual task, so we employ contractors on Upwork (a freelancer website) to locate contacts whose e-mails have bounced. For low volumes, expect to pay about $1 per contact; at scale, the cost is much lower. Our contractors find new contact information for 68 percent of our former clients.

Indirect Referrals

Current customers are often the *best* source of referrals, but they are not the *only* source. Particularly in B2B, a customer's social sphere is limited to colleagues and vendors; customers are unlikely to know and highly unlikely to provide references to their counterpart at a competitor. When the direct route doesn't work, there is an effective indirect route. First, ask a customer to connect you with their other favorite vendors or partners. Then, simply trade leads informally or formally (via affiliate marketing) with complementary suppliers. Finally, include employees across the company in lead referral programs.

Best Practices for Referrals

The best referral programs are characterized by the following:

- *Simplicity*: Make everything about the referral program simple and easy, including communications, landing pages, and forms.

- *Transparency*: Provide transparency at the beginning, middle, and end of the referral process. At the beginning, share details about how the referral process will work, and convey the program's benefits for the customer and the referral. Include the customer in the cc or bcc (with disclosure) in the first e-mail communication with the referred lead. During the process, provide the customer with the means to check referral status. Finally, provide closure to the customer whether the deal results in a win or a loss.

- *Incentives*: Provide appropriate monetary and/or nonmonetary incentives to both the customer and the referred lead. Incentives should not be so large as to be judged a bribe and must comply with applicable laws and with the customer's business ethics policies. In most cases, this means monetary rewards should be less than $100 per referral. Quite often, nonmonetary incentives are a better choice, especially those tied directly to the product or service (for example, beta tests, priority support, or added features). Donations to charity are another compelling option.

As with all initiatives, the success of a referral program depends on having expectations set, activities calendared, and performance measured. To that end, we recommend leveraging referral software solutions as part of your prospecting mix and assigning a partial or full resource from sales operations or marketing to the program.

Though it falls into the "simplicity" category, we have saved the ultimate referral best practice for last. Most salespeople approach referral requests in an open-ended way. However, there is a simple way to increase your odds of success and make it easy for your prospects to help. Check your client's LinkedIn profile and identify three to five connections that you want to engage as prospects. Then ask your client for permission to mention him or her in your communications to the prospect. It truly is that simple.

Executing Multitouch, Multichannel Prospecting Campaigns

After advancing quality leads from the New Queue into the Working Queue, sales professionals work to set up first meetings with responsive prospects. The goal of the first meeting, especially with complex B2B sales, is not necessarily full-blown qualification; rather, the goal is to determine "Are we a fit?" and set up next steps leading to a qualified lead following one or more discussions with the one or more decision makers and influencers involved in the deal.

The first decision to make in a Predictable Prospecting campaign is the choice of communication channels. Since social media direct messaging is not yet a proven or accepted B2B channel, let's focus on e-mail and telephone. Although we would like to say there is a universal magic mix, like many other things, it is context dependent, and it must be continually optimized through testing and iterating.

We cannot tell you what perfect looks like, but we can share what actual industry standards look like thanks to a study[7] conducted by SalesStaff, a B2B appointment setting service provider. Within a one-hour window, the company filled out "Contact Us" forms on the websites of 350 B2B companies. In addition

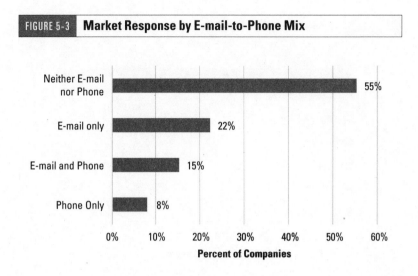

FIGURE 5-3   **Market Response by E-mail-to-Phone Mix**

Source: SalesStaff, http://salesstaff.com/market-research-survey/.

to standard contact information, SalesStaff included a message indicating "a project existed where the target company may be of use." The mix of responses is shown in Figure 5-3.

The actual market response is definitely *not* what great looks like. A shocking majority of B2B companies completely ignore valuable inbound leads. The good news for B2B sales professionals is that it should be easy to stand out with a multichannel campaign when only 15 percent of competitors respond via both e-mail and phone.

And what about multitouch? The same SalesStaff study revealed, as shown in Figure 5-4, that the vast majority of companies that respond via e-mail do so only once. The overall average is fewer than two e-mails.

The data is only slightly better for the 23 percent of companies that respond via phone. As shown in Figure 5-5, most companies give up after two call attempts.

FIGURE 5-4   **Market Response by Number of E-mail Touches**

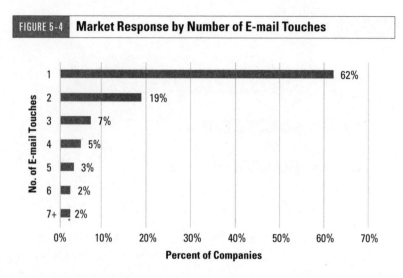

Source: SalesStaff, http://salesstaff.com/market-research-survey/.

FIGURE 5-5   **Market Response by Number of Phone Touches**

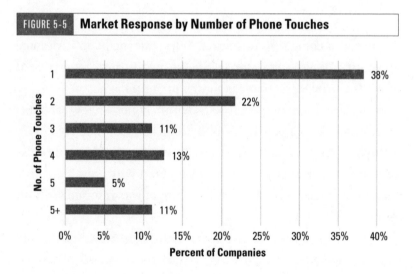

Source: SalesStaff, http://salesstaff.com/market-research-survey/.

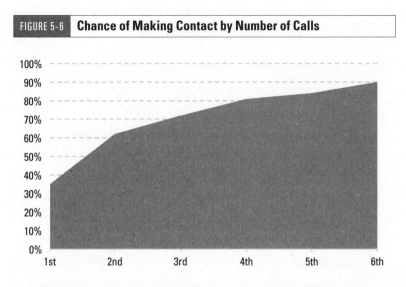

FIGURE 5-6   **Chance of Making Contact by Number of Calls**

Source: InsideSales.com, http://static.insidesales.com/assets/pdf/ebook-the-art-of-cold-calling-and-the
-science-of-contact-ratios.pdf.

What makes this most shocking is that sales professionals have long known (via the InsideSales.com and MIT study cited earlier) that persistence in the follow-up pays. As shown in Figure 5-6, toughing it out for six calls instead of one can increase the chances of making contact from the mid-30s to as high as 90 percent! For reference, the average company that made calls attempted contact only three times.

The average company fails to respond adequately to inbound leads. Among those that do, only 15 percent leverage a multi-channel strategy reliant on phone and e-mail. Assuming the overall averages hold, those multichannel companies persist for five touches, including two e-mails and three calls.

A Sample Outbound Campaign

While we want to avoid providing a universal prescription, we do want to set a recommended starting point that sales teams can confidently use to build multichannel, multitouch campaigns. There are all kinds of salespeople. Some are hunters with the luxury of being either purely inbound or purely outbound. Others have a mix of inbound and outbound responsibilities. In the most complex, but by no means unusual, scenario, a sales professional must be adept at balancing everything, including hunting, farming, servicing, and renewing.

Consequently, each type of salesperson will possess unique abilities to execute time-light e-mail touches and time-intensive phone touches. To that end, the following sample campaign takes a middle-of-the road approach to Predictable Prospecting, and it recommends 8 to 12 touches over 22 business days, or a calendar month. This sample outbound campaign includes 9 touches over 20 business days, including seven e-mails and two phone calls as illustrated in Table 5-4. We will comment as we go regarding adjustments that should be made for inbound response campaigns. For simplicity, we will continue with the CMO example we began in the previous chapter, repeated here for convenience:

For whom? Chief marketing officers at B2B information technology companies headquartered in the United States with revenues of $1 billion to $6 billion

To do what? Increase inbound lead generation

In order to? Increase the revenue impact from marketing at a 5 times or greater ROI.

By what means? Content syndication on third-party websites

TABLE 5-4	Nine-Touch, 20-Business-Day Outbound Campaign

DAY	TOUCH TYPE	CONTENT	CALL TO ACTION (CTA)
1	E-mail (1)	None	Internal referral
2	E-mail (2)	Reference to survey	Internal referral
3	E-mail (3)	Infographic	Aware asset click
8	E-mail (4)	None	Secure meeting
8	Call with voice mail	None	Reply to e-mail (4)
11	E-mail (5)	Diagnostic tool	Interested asset click
13	E-mail (6)	Product demo video	Evaluating asset click
18	E-mail (7)	"Breakup"	Test for any interest
20	Call with voice mail	None	Reply to e-mail (7)

For those wanting a shorter and more delicate campaign, we offer one with three e-mails and five calls over 13 business days as shown in Table 5-5. Among the five calls in this campaign, the salesperson only leaves two voice mails—one at the beginning and one at the end.

TABLE 5-5	Eight-Touch, 13-Business-Day Outbound Campaign

DAY	TOUCH TYPE	CONTENT	CALL TO ACTION
1	E-mail (1)	None	Internal referral
1	Call with voice mail (1)	None	Reply to e-mail (1)
4	Call, no voice mail (2)	None	Secure meeting
7	E-mail (2)	Infographic	Aware asset click
7	Call, no voice mail (3)	None	Secure meeting
10	Call, no voice mail (4)	None	Secure meeting
13	E-mail (3)	"Breakup"	Test for any interest
13	Call with voice mail (5)	None	Reply to e-mail (3)

In the remainder of this chapter, we will explain the templates used in the more comprehensive campaign detailed in Table 5-4.

Starting with Precadence Planning

Precadence planning is our term for a light version of precall planning optimized for low- to moderate-volume, multitouch campaigns. At the Rainmaker 2016 conference in Atlanta, SalesLoft CEO Kyle Porter shared just how important precadence planning has become. (The company applied an algorithm to classify each of the 4 million e-mails its SDR users sent to prospects as either generic or personalized. In their experiment, *generic* meant templates with or without dynamic fields such as first name or company name. The personalized e-mails had to have distinct subject lines or at least a sentence of unique text in the body. SalesLoft found prospects replied to 2.7 percent of generic e-mails and to 8.0 percent of personalized e-mails. Given that generic e-mail delivery rates (due to ever-improving spam filters) and open rates are collapsing by the hour, it behooves every SDR to personalize their cadences.

The key, of course, is striking the balance between too much and too little research given the fact only 1 in 20, give or take, prospects will schedule are-we-a-fit calls in response to outbound cadences. In contrast to the catchy but impractical 3×3 approach (3 things in 3 minutes), we feel a good balance is trying to learn no more than two contextually relevant pieces of information about a prospect in 10 minutes or less. Stop and move on after you gather two pieces of information or you hit the 10-minute mark, whichever comes first. Also, remember to log the information in your CRM so that you (or your SDR descendants) don't have to reinvent the wheel.

The first piece of information should be about the prospects as individuals. For B2B sales, seek professional information starting with LinkedIn and possibly Twitter. If the prospects are public enough, you may find news about them by searching the

Internet with a combination of their name and company. In the event you cannot find professional information, you may seek out personal information on LinkedIn, Facebook, and other social networks. Tread lightly with personal information because being approached by a stranger (yes, SDR, that's you) with personal information can be off-putting. If you go this route, focus on genuinely shared interests and hobbies about which are you prepared to speak at length.

The second piece of information should be about the prospect's company. To find a strategic initiative aligned to your solution, comb though press releases, financial releases including 10Ks and 10Qs, and investor presentations.

Touch 1, Day 1, E-mail, Call to Action (CTA): Internal Referral

From: <rep_e-mail_address>

Subject: Potential Lead Generation Partnership

Hi <Prospect_First_Name>,

I'm just checking in to see if you are the person responsible for lead generation at <Prospect_Company_Name>. If you aren't the right person to contact, can you please forward me on to someone more appropriate?

Please advise,

<Rep_First_Name> <Rep_Last_Name>
<Rep_Phone_Number>

Designed as a find-the-right-person e-mail, the first touch applies a number of best practices. The sender is a real person, the sales executive. The subject is descriptive of the body of the e-mail and applies the first-word-capitalized best practice we shared in the previous chapter. In addition, the word "Potential" kindles loss aversion; people do not want to miss out on valuable opportunities. The body is extremely short. The risk we took in not including any problem-solution or company-specific language should pay off since our goal is to confirm responsibility or get an internal referral. In this case, we could hit the jackpot if the CMO replies and copies his direct report in charge of demand generation. The closing, "Please advise," has been proven recently to command a higher response rate than more conventional ones such as "Thank you," "Regards," "Sincerely," or "Cordially." Finally, the sales professional's signature does not include her company's website to maintain the integrity of the one e-mail/one call-to-action rule.

Sending a find-the-right-person e-mail to a person *senior* to or *lateral* to your target prospect can be particularly effective. We were once on the receiving end of this strategy. The first e-mail sent to one of our bosses was as follows:

From: <rep_e-mail_address>

Subject: Sales Messaging at <Prospect_Company>

<Prospect_First_Name>,

If you are focused on driving growth in 2016 through new sales messaging at <Prospect_Company>, our firm could potentially help.

Through our <product>, <Company_Name> specializes in equipping B2B salespeople to <value_proposition>.

Clients including <companies_similar_to_prospect_company>, partner with <Company_Name> to create <deliverables>.

(continued)

I would be happy to share <specific_work_samples> that have led to consistent results.

Is the timing right for a brief meeting regarding 2016 priorities?

Best,

<Rep_First_Name>

After receiving no reply to the first e-mail, the salesperson sent the following (take special note of the subject line and body personalization):

From: <rep_e-mail_address>

Subject: Should I Contact Jeremey Donovan?

<Prospect_First_Name>,

You may or may not have seen the e-mail below. As you consider whether a conversation with <Company_Name> makes sense based on current <Prospect_Company> priorities, I wanted to provide additional background to help determine if there is any relevancy.

Recent client scenario: <Company_Name> was engaged by <company_similar_to prospect_company> to <value_proposition_with_link_to_case_study>.

<Short_description_of_the_case_study_including_ROI-focused_outcome.>

If you would like to learn more about <product>, please send a quick reply and we can set up a short web meeting.

If someone like Jeremey Donovan is a better contact for these topics, please send me in the right direction.

Best,

<Rep_First_Name>

The salesperson actually sent that series of two e-mails to a large number of people (perhaps too many) across the firm. Nearly everyone forwarded the second e-mail after receiving it, and we called the sender to discuss both his prospecting approach and his product.

Touch 2, Day 3, E-mail, CTA: Internal Referral

From: <rep_e-mail_address>

Subject: Re: Potential Lead Generation Partnership

Hi <Prospect_First_Name>,

Hope you're doing well! Just wanted to shoot you a quick note to follow up on my e-mail from the other day.

We recently surveyed 500 CMOs at information technology companies about their marketing strategies. The survey has revealed that the No. 1 priority for marketing leaders is increasing the number of inbound leads. However, only 10 percent of those same leaders felt their programs were highly successful.

Are you the right person to share the survey results with? If not, can you please refer me to the person in charge of lead generation?

Thanks,

<Rep_First_Name>

Hi <Prospect_First_Name>,

I'm just checking in to see if you are the person responsible for lead generation at <Prospect_Company_Name>. If you aren't the right person to contact, can you please forward me on to someone more appropriate?

Please advise,

<Rep_First_Name> <Rep_Last_Name>
<Rep_Phone_Number>

Touch 2 includes a number of incremental best practices starting with the use of "Re:" in the subject line. While in-line replies are highly effective, the technique must be used sparingly and genuinely. In the entire campaign, we use this only once to prevent the thread from getting too long. Additionally, overusing "Re:" is as off-putting as overusing someone's first name during a conversation. We have received plenty of e-mails out of the blue with "Re:" or "Fw:". The worst, albeit clever, offense we came across while collecting unsolicited e-mails was the following:

From: <rep1_e-mail_address>

Subject: <Prospect_First_Name> Meet <Rep2_First_Name>

Hey <Prospect_First_Name>,

I came across you on LinkedIn and noticed we have some mutuals like <Person1_In_Prospect_Network>, and <Person2_In_Prospect_Network>. I'm based in <Rep1_Location>, but <Rep2_First_Name> from our team is in <Prospect_Location> next week and would love to meet.

Best,

<Rep1_First_Initial>

This e-mail was followed a mere three minutes later by the following:

From: <rep2_e-mail_address>

Subject: Re: <Prospect_First_Name> Meet <Rep2_First_Name>

Thanks, <Rep1_First_Name>.

Great to meet, <Prospect_First_Name>. Would be great to find some time to meet. I will be in <Prospect_Location> from <Dates> (next week). When might suit you?

For a little bit of context, we run the <Conference_Name>, Europe's leading <Industry> conference, alongside a number of leading conferences in North America and Asia. Some press on our flagship event below.

Best,

<Rep2_First_Name>

We looked up Rep1 and Rep2 on LinkedIn, and they did at least appear to be real people. Moreover, Rep1 was indeed a second-degree contact to the author who received the e-mail and was connected to the shared individuals (mostly LIONs— LinkedIn Open Networkers) referenced. Nonetheless, the whole thing felt disingenuous since it did not come from a first-degree contact, was too fast, did not include Rep1 in the cc line of Rep2's reply, and did not include the text of the first e-mail in the second e-mail. Yes, salespeople have to sell. However, ethics wins in a relationship-driven world. Sales guru Zig Ziglar said it best, "You can have everything in life you want, if you will just help other people get what they want."

Returning to the Predictable Prospecting touch 2 e-mail, the body maintains the same call to action as touch 1 to keep the conversation genuine and begins the problem-solution journey we previewed in the last chapter. Importantly, each e-mail should contain not only a single call to action but also a single pain point or value proposition.

Finally, the closing of touch 2 could have used "Please advise" again, but we decided to mix things up with "Thanks." In addition, we close with only the salesperson's first name since real people tend to reply with less formality.

Touch 3, Day 6, E-mail, CTA: Unaware to Aware Asset Click

From: <rep_e-mail_address>

Subject: Lead Generation Infographic

Hi <Prospect_First_Name>,

We just synthesized a number of lead generation best practices from the CMO Survey I mentioned last week into an infographic.

The survey revealed that next-generation content assets like infographics, videos, and e-books are outperforming traditional assets like white papers and blogs. However, most CMOs are struggling to shift resources to the newer, more effective options.

Check out more about content marketing and other lead generation best practices by viewing the infographic.

Thanks,

<Rep_First_Name> <Rep_Last_Name>
<Rep_Phone_Number>

Assuming no response after the first two touches, we remain optimistic that our contact is responsible for lead generation in his organization but, as yet, is just not motivated to reply. In touch 3, we are in hot pursuit of a click that will serve as a signpost validating that the prospect is aware he has a problem. Here we pick from our list of short, high-value, vendor-agnostic content types such as short videos, blog posts, and infographics. Once again, we have one problem-solution and one call to action. In addition, we have loaded this e-mail with psychological triggers. "We *just* synthesized" appeals to the human craving for newness. The repeated phrase "best practices" serves as social proof that is far more powerful than a vendor's own findings.

Touch 4, Day 8, E-mail, CTA: Secure a Meeting

From: <rep_e-mail_address>

Subject: Lead Generation Insights

Hi <Prospect_First_Name>,

I'm a solutions advisor with <Rep_Company_Name>. We work with companies like <Prospect_Competitor_1> and <Prospect_Competitor_2> to help them increase the return on investment of their lead generation programs.

Do you have 15 minutes to chat next week about how we have helped organizations like yours? We'll know right away if it's something that makes sense for <Prospect_Company>.

Please e-mail me with a date and time that works, and I'll send you a meeting request.

Thanks,

<Rep_First_Name> <Rep_Last_Name>
<Rep_Phone_Number>

After providing value with nothing in return during the prior two touches, we have earned the right to ask for a meeting in touch 4. By mentioning competitors (that a company really *does* do business with), we trigger curiosity and desire. Our call to action imposes very little burden on the prospect by asking for just 15 minutes and by promising to set up the meeting request.

Touch 5, Day 8, Phone, CTA: Secure a Meeting

Hi <Prospect_First_Name>,

This is <Rep_First_Name> with <Rep_Company_Name>. I sent you a few e-mails lately on a CMO survey we recently completed. Like most of our clients, I'm guessing you are pretty busy so I figured I'd reach out to you to see if you wanted me to walk through some of the findings and explore how we might work together.

If you have time for a quick call, just reply back to the e-mail I sent earlier today or give me a ring.

Again, it's <Rep_First_Name> <Rep_Last_Name> at <Rep_Phone_Number>.

Take care.

In this campaign, we wait until the fifth touch to call for two reasons. First, a sales professional should figure out if the contact is even the right person before devoting time to calling. Second, as mentioned in our commentary for touch 4, the salesperson has to set the expectation that the prospect will get value out of the relationship by giving before the prospect asks—relying on the psychological principle of reciprocity.

Notably, we have decided to conduct the touch 5 phone call the same day as but just after the touch 4 e-mail. This recently discovered best practice relies on the familiarity benefit of the recent impression—the prospect is more likely to recognize the name on the caller identification. Touch 5 also makes the ask, replying to an e-mail, a much less burdensome task compared to returning a phone call.

On a related side note, prospects are as much as 57.8 percent more likely[8] to pick up calls coming from their area code compared to blocked, long-distance, or toll-free numbers. While many dialer technology companies provide this feature, known as *local presence*, tread cautiously because the practice amounts to starting out what one hopes will blossom into a meaningful, long-term relationship with a lie. If you do adopt local presence, role-play to ensure that SDRs are comfortable explaining the practice when called out on it. For example, an effective and honest response is, "Our company uses a telephony provider that dynamically provisions phone numbers."

Voice mail scripts, such as the one above, should be written conversationally using less formal language and short sentences. Even better, consider drafting voice mail recommendations as bullets. For example:

- *Greeting:* Hyperpersonalized

- *Benefit:* Offer to walk through CMO survey findings

- *Call to action:* Reply to e-mail to set up time

We strongly recommend that sales professionals practice the script to internalize it rather than memorize it. Furthermore, to sound more friendly and authentic, we encourage salespeople to stand up and smile while leaving voice mails.

A salesperson will connect live with a prospect 20 to 30 percent of the time; the rate is even higher for rapid response (defined as less than 5 minutes) to inbound leads. In the happy event of reaching a person on a cold call, especially in complex B2B selling situations, we urge salespeople to resist the temptation to qualify the prospect then and there. Instead, they should use those precious moments to set up a meeting to further explore their situation and needs.

It is not dialing that makes salespeople dislike cold calling. It is connecting. Invariably, the prospect at the other end of the line regrets answering the phone as soon as she picks up. To make the proactive outreach call better for both parties, we recommend that the salesperson have a set of talking points covering the following four areas. (Though we do not recommend scripting live calls, we scripted the talking points below to make this example more concrete. Just make sure to cover items 1 through 4.)

1. Introduction (Let's make a deal.)
    - Hi, Betty? (wait for response)
    - I'm Wilma from SalesCo. I lead our practice serving product managers at financial services companies.
    - I appreciate that you were not expecting my call, but let me borrow two minutes of your time. If you think we might work together, we can schedule a follow-up call. If not, you can go on with your day. (Alternative: I just want to make sure I'm calling the right person at PropsectCo. Are you responsible for new product development?)

2. Show me that you know me.
    - I just reviewed the transcript of ProspectCo's most recent earnings call and noticed that your CEO has committed to increasing the percentage of revenue

from new products introduced in the last 18 months.
- Did I understand that right? (wait for answer)

3. Value pitch
   - At SalesCo, we help product managers at financial services companies implement agile new product development practices by providing a software platform along with services and training.
   - In fact, we just helped another Fortune 50 financial services company increase its percentage of revenue from new products to 30 percent from 20 percent.

4. Objective
   - Since I'm assuming you are really busy right now, can we schedule a 10-minute call to discuss your business and some ideas I'd like to share?

Let's closely examine this call flow starting with the introduction. The first words, "Hi, Betty?" are pretty standard. Besides drawing upon the timeless practice of engaging people by using their first name, it is also possible that one has the wrong number for a prospect. Once the prospect confirms, we intentionally *do not* respond with the cliché "How are you doing today?" Instead, we launch right in with "I'm Wilma from SalesCo. I lead our practice serving product managers at large financial services companies."

Importantly, we use the phrase "I lead" to convey a sense of authority. Everyone leads something so do not be afraid to say it. And, while a salesperson might lead a broader practice, we narrowed it down to the precise role of the prospect, a product manager at a large financial services company.

We end the introduction with, "I appreciate that you were not expecting my call, but let me borrow two minutes of your time. If you think we might work together, we can schedule a follow-up call. If not, you can go on with your day," instead of asking, "Do you have a quick minute to talk?" or "Did I catch you at a good time?" This wording is important because we do not want to give the prospect the chance to say, "Well, no actually. I've got to run to a meeting. Bye." Here is a great variation: "Let's make a deal. We chat for two minutes. I'll briefly share what my company does and ask you one question about how you manage (prospect's key objective). Then you decide whether or not we should continue the discussion in a follow-up call. OK?"

The first 5 to 15 seconds are always the most tense because rejection is always uncomfortable and prospects always have their guard up. Greetings such as "How are you doing today?" have become ineffective. However, this approach was once quite effective because it was an unconventionally informal way to address prospects. Salespeople are ever on the hunt for effective *pattern interrupts*—that is, in this context, conversation starters that disrupt a prospect's behavioral pattern for rejecting unsolicited calls.[9] A couple of fresh ones to emerge include "I'm guessing I caught you at a bad time. What were you doing?" and "How do you typically handle cold calls?" A particularly interesting one we heard at a conference[10] was "Are you sure you want to do that?" in response to the "Please send me an e-mail" objection. Of course, today's killer pattern interrupt will become tomorrow's cliché as it gains popularity in the sales community.

Most prospects expect salespeople to launch right into a pitch. We confound their expectations with the "show me that you know me" step. In our example, we referenced a relevant insight from a recent earnings transcript. We also could have cited other professional information gleaned from annual reports, press releases, websites, or LinkedIn. There are, of course, other ways to prove that you care about earning a prospect's business and that you have invested time up front to do so. Since we like pairing calls with e-mails, we might say, "I recently sent you an e-mail referencing a study we did on product management. Did you get that?" To which the prospect might reply, "Yeah, I might have, but I don't remember," which gives the salesperson the chance to provide a one-sentence summary. Finally, if we have nothing else, then we try to refer to a personal intersection gleaned from social media such as a common connection or hobby. Hoping to get the prospect to engage, we end the "show me that you know me" step by asking for confirmation: "Did I understand that right?" Since any response is a good response, welcome any corrections the prospect makes to your analysis.

In as little as one minute into the call, the sales professional has earned the right to *very briefly* pitch the value of her solution to the prospect. A great value statement leads with the benefit (the why) the prospect will receive—"At SalesCo, we help product managers at financial services companies implement agile new product development practices." The benefit should be stated at the level relevant to the prospect as determined by your Ideal Prospect Persona. Here, we used "implement agile new product development practices." However, if we were speaking to the CEO, we would frame it at a higher level: "increase revenue from new products." After sharing why we do what we do, we explain how we do it: "by providing a software platform along with services and training." Then we conclude the value pitch step with relevant proof in the form of a very high level case study: "In fact, we just helped another Fortune 50 financial services company increase its percentage of revenue from new products to 30 percent from 20 percent." Social proof is extremely effective since it triggers loss aversion; people do not want to be left out of an opportunity or left behind their competitors.

Finally, we move to the objective. Every call and every meeting needs to have an objective. In most business-to-business selling situations, attempting a one-call close is ill advised. Instead, our objective is to secure a meeting. We acknowledge that the prospect is busy, ask for just 10 minutes to accomplish two things: discuss *his* business and share some of *our* ideas. This shows we are not out to present a standard pitch deck to them; rather, we are curious about his business and interested in having a true dialogue to determine if we are a fit.

(Though rare, going for the close does work sometimes. For instance, we ran across a firm that sells Internet services to single-location restaurants that not only gives owners their own website but also integrates that website with popular dining review sites like Yelp. When the price is low enough, the owner busy enough, and the value proposition high enough, a one-call close works well.)

One should expect objections. Here is how we would respond to the most common ones:

- *Objection*: I'm really busy right now.
  Response: I know you are busy, so I'll be brief.

- *Objection*: Can you call me back next week (or next month)?
  Response: Sure. Let's put a time on the calendar to reconnect. Would (specific time) on (specific day) work for you?

- *Objection*: OK, why don't you send me some information via e-mail and I'll have a look.
  Response: Sure, I'll send you some information. Since we have a lot of material, can you give me an idea of what might be most helpful? *Followed by*: And let's schedule a quick follow-up call since people find it more valuable to hear how this works given their specific needs.

- *Objection:* We already have an internal (or external) solution.
  Response: That's excellent since many of our clients find that
  we complement the great tools they already have. Which
  ones are you using?

- *Objection:* I have no budget.
  Response: Understood. I'm really just looking to have an
  introductory conversation and don't expect you to have
  budget right now. I'd like to understand your needs. If you
  see value after we meet, then I can partner with you to bring
  the opportunity to your colleagues.

- *Objection:* This sounds expensive.
  Response: Yes, I completely understand. I'm focused on my
  clients' return on investment. Let's take time to figure out
  if this might be valuable first. Then we can talk about price.
  (*Note:* The previous sentence is also the answer to someone
  who asks about price too early.) *Or ask:* Is this a value issue
  or a budget issue?

At a high level, the responses above follow the golden rule of
improvisational comedy: "Yes, and . . ." More specifically, objection handling follows a general pattern. First, pause briefly to
think. Even though the silence may feel awkward to you, the
prospect either will not notice or will appreciate that you are
taking the time to process what he said. Second, acknowledge
the objection with empathy. To acknowledge does not necessarily
mean to agree; it means to understand. In certain circumstances,
saying, "That is a great question" works well. Third, ask probing
questions to isolate the issue. Consider asking, "Why do you feel
that way?" Fourth, handle the isolated objection. While there are
many ways to do this (entire books have been written on the
subject), our go-to approach is to share a specific case study of a

similar client with the same objection who realized significant value. Fifth and finally, confirm that you have addressed the prospect's concern. Ask, "Did I answer your question fully?" Then pause. You need to make sure the objection is closed so that it does not linger in the prospect's mind and resurface.

If a prospect pushes back three times, then we relent and move into referral mode: "It sounds like you are really busy, or I may not have done a great job of explaining how we can help you. Is there someone on your team I could speak with who could report back to you?"

Touch 6, Day 11, E-mail, CTA: Aware to Interested Asset Click

and

Touch 7, Day 13, E-mail, CTA: Interested to Evaluating Asset Click

Touches 6 and 7 are identical in construction to touch 3 so we will not draw out this chapter with e-mail templates. Instead, we summarize what each touch needs to accomplish.

Touch 6 serves as a signpost indicating that the prospect has progressed to the interested stage. Like touch 3, this touch frames a problem-solution (via obstacle, outcome, and opportunity) and drives a call to action in the form of an asset click. However, this time the content served up might be a topical report, e-book, diagnostic tool, or thematic webinar. It is also appropriate for the salesperson to gently begin to develop awareness of her company and its products.

Touch 7 serves as a signpost indicating the prospect may be evaluating the salesperson's company and its products. This is the opportunity to share case studies, testimonials, product reviews, product demo videos, and product comparison charts. Time permitting, the salesperson should lightly customize the e-mail to demonstrate research on and awareness of the prospect's company and the specific business challenges it faces.

Touch 8, Day 18, E-mail, CTA: Secure a Meeting

and

Touch 9, Day 20, Phone, CTA: Secure a Meeting

Touches 8 and 9 are a complementary pair like touches 4 and 5, albeit with differences in the timing gap and in content. The final two touches execute what is colloquially known as a "Hail Mary" or "breakup," giving the prospect one last chance to reply. Here we wait two days between touches rather than doing them on the same day to let the feeling of lost opportunity sink in.

From: <rep_e-mail_address>

Subject: Follow-up

<Prospect_First_Name>,

I have been trying to connect with you over the past two weeks to explore ways <Rep_Company> can help increase the ROI of your lead generation programs. Since I have not heard back from you, I'm left to draw a few possible conclusions:

1. You are all set with lead generation partners, and if that is the case, please reply with "1" so that I stop bothering you.

(continued)

> 2. You are interested in what <Rep_Company> can do, but you are just very busy right now. If this is the case, please reply with "2."
>
> 3. You got attacked by a lemur and want me to call for help. If that is the case, please reply with "3."
>
> Please advise,
>
> <Rep_First_Name> <Rep_Last_Name>
> <Rep_Phone_Number>

In case you think option 3 is not real, it is from an actual e-mail received by one of the authors. In fact, the e-mail even included a very cute photograph of said animal. Since that was a last-ditch effort, the salesperson had little to lose and a lot to gain by adding a touch of humor. We quite like the reply with "1," "2," or "3" which makes it incredibly easy for the prospect to engage.

If the above e-mail does not suit your fancy, here is one that is a little more formal yet carries a tone of self-pity. Also, notice we switched the closing from "Please advise" to "Just let me know either way," which at least one of our clients has found to be effective.

> From: <rep_e-mail_address>
>
> Subject: Follow-up
>
> <Prospect_First_Name>,
>
> I have been trying to connect with you over the past two weeks to explore ways <Rep_Company> can help increase the ROI of your lead generation programs.
>
> Since I have not heard back from you, I'm afraid I have done a poor job of showing you the value we can offer as a partner. We have made great strides helping our clients increase lead volumes and win rates.

(continued)

Let's schedule a 5- to 10-minute call so that I can understand your lead generation needs. When are you free to talk?

Just let me know either way,

<Rep_First_Name> <Rep_Last_Name>
<Rep_Phone_Number>

Using Social Selling Tools Tactfully

You likely noticed that all of the touches we walked through relied on phone and e-mail. What about engaging prospects via social media channels?

For starters, we think social media is more valuable as a research tool than as an outreach tool. LinkedIn and, to a lesser extent, Twitter are valuable for discovering professional interests and mutual connections. Those two channels plus Facebook also provide a glimpse into your prospects' personal and social interests. Given how much it is possible to learn about people from their digital tracks, remember to exercise restraint so as not to be off-putting.

We find solicitations via social media, including and especially LinkedIn, highly irritating. Following the "advise unto others as you would advise unto yourself" mantra, we recommend using LinkedIn with a light touch. Following SalesLoft's best practice (mentioned elsewhere in the book), consider waiting to connect on LinkedIn until after you have received an e-mail reply or reached the person on the phone. And when you do connect, replace LinkedIn's standard "I'd like to join your LinkedIn network" invitation with personalized text. As long as you are not selling or asking for a meeting, connecting on LinkedIn at the middle or end of a cadence is an acceptable next-best practice.

We recommend spending 30 to 60 minutes per day establishing a professional presence on social media. Blog, share, answer questions, and comment thoughtfully on others' contributions, particularly those of your ideal prospects. Additionally, spend time polishing your LinkedIn profile because prospects will check you out to see if they can trust you. Some of the more important elements of the profile include your photo, your professional headline, your skills, and especially your recommendations. Avoid boasting of your sales acumen, and instead focus on the value you bring to clients. Last, with respect to recommendations, give and ye shall receive.

––––––––––

Even with increasingly impressive out-of-the-box functionality available from most CRM vendors, no human being could successfully execute overlapping, multichannel, multitouch campaigns. Fortunately, an ecosystem of workflow tools has emerged that integrates seamlessly with most major platforms. For the Working Queue, our clients have had success with three in particular: InsideSales.com, Salesloft Cadence, and Velocify.

If the prospect does not reply after all this work, the contact should be moved to the No Response or Interest contact status and put back into a slow-drip nurturing cycle for (re-)activation.

However, if the prospect does reply and a first meeting is scheduled, the salesperson should advance the contact status to Qualifying, the subject of the next chapter.

(Dis-) Qualifying Prospects

After spending a massive, thankless, and often frustrating amount of work just to secure a first conversation, one might *not* expect a salesperson's call objective to be to disqualify the prospect! Remember, Predictable Prospecting is a top-of-the-funnel process designed to identify the highest-value prospects—those with a high profit potential *and* a high probability of becoming a customer. The time, effort, and money spent futilely pursuing unqualified prospects is better invested elsewhere.

The Predictable Prospecting approach calls for two waves of qualification (we are dropping the "dis-" going forward since the message is clear): are we a fit? (AWAF) analysis and budget, authority, need, and timing (BANT) analysis.

AWAF

The initial wave of qualification is called *are we a fit?* (AWAF), and it should be completed in an initial 15-minute call. At least two bad situations can happen in sales prospecting. First, as cited earlier, a salesperson can pursue prospects who endlessly string them along. Second, a salesperson can sign up a customer who does not get sufficient value and therefore does not renew, and, possibly, becomes a vocal detractor. In many ways, the second is more destructive than the first. The salesperson might get her commission, but at the risk of her reputation and that of her company.

To avoid either of these traps, every sales team must have a set of (no more than five) must-have criteria that is based, unsurprisingly, on the known characteristics of "bad prospects" and "bad customers." AWAF criteria useful in qualifying prospects include physical or technology infrastructure, regulatory requirements, and cultural compatibility. For example, it would be useless trying to sell A4 paper (8.27 inches by 11.69 inches) to a company that has printers accommodating only U.S. letter paper (8.5 inches by 11.0 inches). The same is true if trying to sell Apache-compatible, Java-based Internet services to a company wedded to a Microsoft .net web server infrastructure. Or illiquid financial derivatives to an investment fund with regulatory risk constraints. AWAF criteria can be any information ruling out a prospect that could not have otherwise been researched in advance.

We often face a major objection to this piece of advice: "What if our solution is strong enough to motivate the prospects to do a forklift upgrade of their people, processes, or technology infrastructure? For instance, what if we demonstrate that it is worth switching from Microsoft to Apache?" As with all such questions, the answer depends on context. If one has a very small territory with very few prospects, then heavy lifting is called for. However, sales professionals are usually more time constrained than territory constrained (though they will never admit it).

Continuing our example, there are nearly 1 billion registered host names, more than 170 million of which are active, being served from more than 5.5 million Internet-facing computers.[1] Since Apache has a 50 percent market share of all active sites, a salesperson with Apache-compatible-only solutions need not bother trying to convert prospects with a significant investment in their Microsoft infrastructure. If you feel strongly that your solution covers a broader range of scenarios, we suggest you build in qualification criteria for each buying scenario. Using the example above, you could have three buying scenarios, each requiring different sets of qualification criteria: (1) *blueprint*—a complete forklift upgrade in the technology; (2) *refresh*—a partial upgrade of older or outdated technology within the existing blueprint; and (3) *project*—a current initiative involving a use case for an upgrade.

In the AWAF call, as in all interactions with prospects, the salesperson acts as a conversation guide. Less experienced salespeople commonly make either one or both of the following mistakes. The first is sticking too literally to both the sequence and the language of the AWAF questions. A more experienced salesperson allows the conversation to flow in a natural manner, starting with confirmatory questions, then subtly shifting to open-ended questions to ensure that all bases are covered. The second mistake concerns failing to get clear answers to all the AWAF questions. Unfortunately, this frequently happens when the salesperson talks too much instead of actively listening, guides too little for the sake of letting the prospects fully express themselves, or is too eager to gather more detailed qualification information.

In order to better guide the AWAF call conversation, many SDRs use a sales presentation or pitch deck. We support this practice, provided that the presentation is prospect centric, short, and high level. Here is a way to pull off this technique with as few as six slides:

Slide 1: The cover slide positions the primary benefit of the product or service. Additionally, the cover slide allows time for introductory pleasantries and for confirmation of the agenda.

Slide 2: If customization is warranted and/or possible (don't guess), then this slide provides an articulation of the prospects' top challenges.

Slide 3: This slide presents solutions to challenges illustrated through one to six use cases.

Slide 4: This slide expresses how the value from the solution will be realized through features and attributes.

Slide 5: If the solution involves product or service options, then this slide provides an overview of the recommended configuration. (For SaaS companies, this would also be the time to conduct a demonstration.)

Slide 6: This slide offers proof that the salesperson's company can deliver value: customer logos, testimonials, independent reviews, and analyst findings.

Assuming she has confirmed a supplier-prospect fit on all the go/no-go questions, the salesperson's goal at the end of the AWAF call is to set up a follow-up phone or face-to-face meeting to kick off the second, more detailed wave of qualification. Always be closing for the next step in the sales process.

Let's look at a specific example of this from Salesforce.com's Data.com business that was used in a pitch to one of the authors.[2] As shown in Figure 6-1, the Data.com presentation began with a cover slide articulating the core value proposition of the product: "Accelerate Your Growth with Data.com." The language is concise and expressed from the perspective of the prospects.

FIGURE 6-1	Data.com Cover Slide

The Data.com presentation did not include a custom slide expressing our top challenges. Though it is possible the salesperson did not feel she knew our issues deeply enough, we suspect corporate policy prevented her from customization. There is always a trade-off at play here. Customized presentations, provided that they are based on adequate discovery, are better because they "show me that you know me." However, allowing sales professionals to customize pitch decks carries two risks. The rarer, and therefore less concerning, of the two is that a salesperson will make false claims about the product in order to get the sale. The greater risk is that account executives will waste massive amounts of time modifying presentations—something we see all the time! With high legal risk aversion and a strong brand, large companies such as Salesforce.com tend to standardize sales presentations.

Data.com's solution slide (Figure 6-2) is one of our favorite slides of all time. During the sales presentation, we spent the bulk of our time on this slide engaged in conversation. We walked through the five use cases, exploring our current approach to each of these sales and marketing processes. Whether we had challenges or were content with our status quo, the Data.com salesperson suggested ways her product could improve our performance. Her tone was that of a partner in our journey, never that of a pushy salesperson.

| FIGURE 6-2 | **Data.com Solution Slide** |

With agreement on the concept of improving our sales and marketing processes, the Data.com salesperson moved on to the features and attributes slide in Figure 6-3. This slide was admittedly busy so the salesperson framed it by explaining that the Data.com solution would enhance both contact and account information. She then followed our lead on how deep we needed to go. We were more focused on sourcing and appending contact information so we spent the bulk of our time there and only touched on account enhancement.

Data.com Features and Attributes Slide

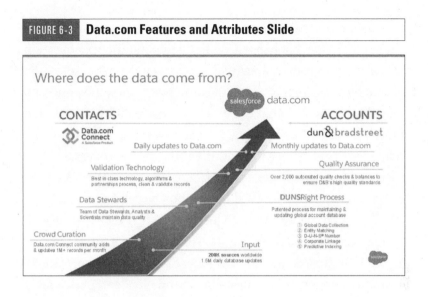

The Data.com solution required the configuration of multiple products in a family. To explain this, the presentation included the slide shown in Figure 6-4.

Data.com Product Options and Configuration Slide

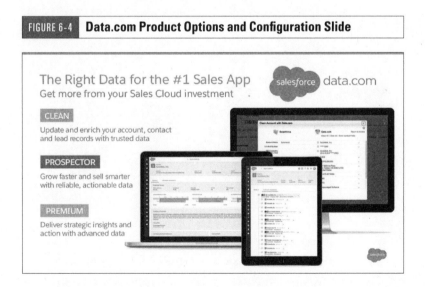

Presentations should be guided conversations, not one-way pitches. To make that happen, each slide should trigger a question that is answered by the next slide. The Data.com presentation started by promising to accelerate our growth. Being skeptics, we thought, "How so?" That question was answered by the solution slide (Figure 6-2) examining our use cases. Our next question, "How will you deliver improvement on those processes?" was answered by the features and attributes slide (Figure 6-3). After that, we wondered, "How will the solution be packaged and sold?" which was answered in the Figure 6-4 slide. Finally, we asked, "What proof do you have that we will get a return on our investment?" The answer, provided in Figure 6-5, set our expectations for improvements as measured by an independent, presumably objective third party.

FIGURE 6-5   **Data.com Proof of Value**

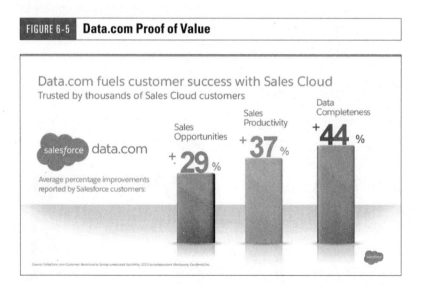

We actually saw two versions of this presentation deck. The original one was much closer to the one represented here. The second version consisted of 12 slides (excluding a legally required safe harbor statement slide at the beginning and a thank-you slide at the end). Because we want to discourage you from creating slides that your salespeople will skip, we will merely describe but not show the slides we removed:

- "Sixth Largest Software Company in the World": This slide included awards, revenues, number of employees, and so on. This one was not completely off the mark, but it served more or less the same purpose as the proof-of-value slide. If you insist on including it, then put it at the end.

- "Become a Customer Company": This was the company's marketing tagline. This did not belong in the presentation and actually disrupted the flow of the story centered on accelerating growth with better data.

- Five slides that went very deeply into the features and attributes of the various products in the family: These were appropriate slides for a second meeting, but not necessarily for a first pitch. Our approach would be to include these in an appendix just in case the conversation goes there.

BANT or ANUM

The second wave of full qualification uses either a methodology, reportedly pioneered by IBM,[3] called BANT (**b**udget, **a**uthority, **n**eed, and **t**ime frame) or ANUM (**a**uthority, **n**eed, **u**rgency, and **m**oney) and takes one or two meetings.

BANT is the most widely adopted sales qualification framework and the one we recommend for Predictable Prospecting. However, since this framework has come under intense fire over the years, we feel the need to defend this choice.

The primary complaint is that B → A → N → T is in the wrong order, and while we agree, we feel its opponents are taking the acronym too literally. Full prospect qualification is an elegant, guided dance during which the conversation will drift in and out of each of the four components. Even the 24 different permutations of the four letters do not do justice to the nonlinear nature of qualification.

Another complaint about BANT is that the specific words constituting the acronym are either too narrow or not narrow enough. Again, we feel the opponents are being too literal. (In our most jaded moments, we think the opponents are simply trying to co-opt and rebrand BANT for their own benefit.) Applying a broader interpretation may help: (1) budget may be expressed as money, funding, spend, or resources; (2) authority may be expressed as control, power, or responsibility; (3) need may be expressed as want, desire, opportunity, pain, challenge, goal, or plan; and (4) time frame may be expressed as urgency, schedule, or prioritization. Countless acronyms besides BANT can be formed by resequencing the first letters of these synonyms.

Establishing the Need

To the extent that a B2B salesperson can control the qualification flow, we recommend starting with need. Synonyms aside, the process for establishing need has become as contentious as the full BANT acronym. One camp supports the mainly reactive approach of listening carefully to discover wants and unmet needs. The other camp promotes the mainly proactive approach of bringing the prospects to the realization of an opportunity they did not know they had. All salespeople recognize this as a false dichotomy, especially in complex transactions, when sales

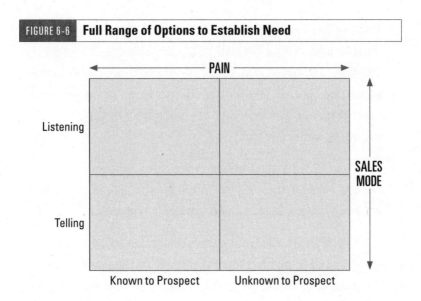

FIGURE 6-6   **Full Range of Options to Establish Need**

professionals constantly shift though the quadrants of Figure 6-6 while uncovering needs *and* suggesting opportunities.

SPIN (**s**ituation, **p**roblem, **i**mplication, **n**eed-payoff) Selling,[4] the most popular need-centric sales methodology, acknowledges these sorts of shifts. Though published in 1988, the book of the same name is just as fresh today as it was the day it was written. At a high level, the key points of the SPIN Selling approach pertaining to full qualification are as follows:

- *Precall planning:* Before the call, write down at least three potential problems that the buyer may have and that your products or services can solve.

- *Preliminaries:* Establish who you are and why you are there, and gain permission to ask questions. Avoid talking about your products and services until late in the process.

- *The S in SPIN:* In the situation phase, ask fact-finding questions to understand the nature of the prospects' business and their key objectives. Critically, these should be questions a salesperson could not have gotten answers to via preliminary research. For instance, "What system or process are you using at present?"

- *The P in SPIN:* In the problem phase, the salesperson uncovers *implied* needs. For example, "What are the biggest challenges you are facing in meeting your strategic objectives?"

- *The I in SPIN:* In the implication phase, the salesperson asks questions designed to increase the size of the problem in the prospects' mind. Great questions include these: "If x is happening, could that lead to an even worse y?" "How long have you had this challenge?" "What are the consequences if you do not solve this challenge?" "What benefits do you expect if you embrace this opportunity?" (*Authors' note:* Avoid implication questions that feel too "slick."). A current twist on implication questioning is the notion of challenging the prospect on predisposed belief systems.

- *The N in SPIN:* Finally, in the need-payoff phase, the salesperson shifts to positive, solution-centered questions designed to have the prospects express an *explicit* need. For example, "How would you find (this solution or benefit) useful in addressing (your explicit need)?"

Though *SPIN Selling* covers most of the bases, *The Challenger Sale* and *The Challenger Customer*, two books by researchers at the Corporate Executive Board (CEB), add an important perspective on how to think about need. (*Note:* The Challenger approach is very much in the proactive camp, arguing that the most effective salespeople bring unexpected insights to customers that increase revenue, lower costs, or control risks.) As reported by the CEB team, the average B2B transaction involves not just 1 but 5.4 decision makers, each with slightly different agendas and risk tolerances.

Think back to our example of a chief marketing officer looking to increase lead generation. Individuals likely to be involved in a purchase decision addressing that need include the CMO, CIO or CTO, CEO, CRO, general counsel, line-of-business leaders, and so on. *The Challenger Customer* highlights consensus building across the group as the main barrier to a successful sale.

To that end, the salesperson needs to find the overarching business challenge the group members share. In fact, the CEB researchers found that selling to individual (lower-level) needs is actually counterproductive once the parties come together. In our example, that means it is a mistake to sell accelerated lead generation to, for example, the CMO, easy technical implementation to the CIO, or cost savings to the CFO. Stepping up a level, these individuals collectively want to increase profitability. The salesperson's job is to prove that among the many options for accomplishing the goal of increasing profit, the supplier's solution is worth the investment of time, effort, and energy.

Confirming the Time Frame

With need established, a salesperson's next order of business, again assuming some degree of control and linearity, is confirming the time frame. Leveraging one of the synonyms for the T in BANT, the salesperson must classify the prospects' sense of urgency as: immediate, high, medium, or low. Organizations that are time limited rather than prospect limited classify only immediate and high as qualified.

Additionally, the salesperson must understand at least three separate but related time frames, including the time to a signed deal; the time to assess, develop, and deploy the solution; and, most important to the prospects, the time to achieve the expected benefits. If the prospects' expectations do not meet the supplier's ability to deliver, either those expectations need to be adjusted or the salesperson needs to flag the prospects as not yet qualified.

Finally, the time frame may involve critical dependencies, most notably, available resources. Independent of budget, there may be insufficient management bandwidth, or there may be other human resources bandwidth constraints that delay the time frame.

By working within a more flexible definition of time frame, you have leeway to ask a range of effective qualification questions:

- What kind of time frame do you have in mind?

- Do you already have a relationship with another supplier or partner? When is the renewal?

- What other suppliers or partners are you considering?

- When was the last time you evaluated a solution to this problem? What was the outcome?

- Where does this rank in your overall priorities?

- What are the consequences if a decision is delayed?

Aggregating the Authority

In this final complaint about the literal interpretation of BANT, the qualification framework assumes a single decision maker with full authority to approve a transaction. While only one person's signature makes it onto a contract, the Corporate Executive

Board (CEB), as previously mentioned, found that an average of 5.4 people are involved in B2B decision making. Hence, knowing who the ultimate decision maker is should not be the sole criterion for checking the box on the A in BANT.

This leaves a sales organization with options that are dependent on the type of deal. In the most complex deals, a lead may be qualified on the basis of need and timing alone. Then the painstaking process of identifying authority becomes part of closing rather than qualification. As an alternative, the salesperson may be expected only to map out the set of individuals involved in making the decision, including titles and names, to meet the authority qualification hurdle. If a salesperson is lucky, an individual prospect in the account may even serve as a guide and share knowledge about what makes her colleagues tick.

Authority questions must be asked with more delicacy than need and time frame questions. Our personal favorites are these:

- In addition to you, who else in your organization is responsible for (will benefit from) solving this problem?

- What does the decision-making process look like at your company for purchases or partnerships like this?

- Who else do you expect will need to be involved in this project? (We doubt anyone asks the direct question, "Are you the final decision maker?"—the most direct, yet still appropriate, question.)

Securing the Budget

In complex B2B transactions, budget, even more than authority, has become less of a qualification criterion, having shifted to being part of the closing process. If a group of prospects with authority in an account have a shared need and high sense of urgency, then they will find the budget to purchase a solution (from the salesperson or her competitor). So, rather than confirming that a budget is available, the salesperson can meet the budget qualification hurdle by knowing the answer to the question, "How will funding for this project be determined?"

If the CFO's name does not come up, the salesperson should bring him up since it is very likely he will be involved. Though a bit more direct, some of the people we work with find success with, "Have you already set aside funds for this project?"

This final question is most appropriate when a salesperson suspects the prospect is already quite far along, possibly at the early stages of vendor selection.

To recap, when sales professionals are more constrained by time than by lead volume, qualification is meant to rapidly convert the most profitable, most likely to close leads into opportunities. Are we a fit? (AWAF) should be accomplished in a 15- to 30-minute phone call. BANT, in whatever permutation applies, should be accomplished in one or two guided conversations of up to one hour each. Leads that are not *yet* qualified should be returned to nurturing with some notes about what made them fall short, along with further intelligence that can be leveraged for mass, data-driven nurturing.

Though sales managers might want to capture all the nitty-gritty details of qualification, it is not practical to do so. If extensive detail were optional, most salespeople would ignore it, and the data would be useless. If extensive detail were required, most salespeople would tacitly rebel, making sure that forms were complete albeit with highly suspect data. We have seen both of these situations more times than we can count. At the end of the day, high-level activity reporting is sufficient. Armed with that data, sales leadership can determine the two metrics that most matter in the qualify stage: the number of touches needed and the time lapse to qualify.

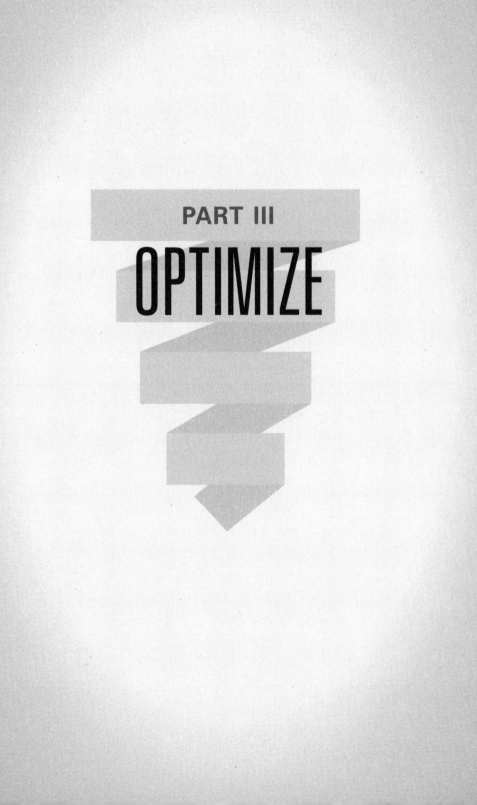

PART III

OPTIMIZE

CHAPTER

7

Measuring and Optimizing Your Pipeline

Prospecting is not a set-it-and-forget-it process. Sales teams must vigilantly measure and optimize their pipeline to achieve the maximum return on sales investment. Over the course of this chapter, we will review the critical metrics that serve as leading and lagging indicators of success at each stage of the sales journey.

Lean Optimization

Since optimization applies to all metrics, we need to spend a little bit of time discussing two extremely popular and closely related techniques. The first, Lean Six Sigma, combines the efficiency principles of the lean movement that started in manufacturing and has since moved on to innovation and other business

FIGURE 7-1	Lean Six Sigma Framework

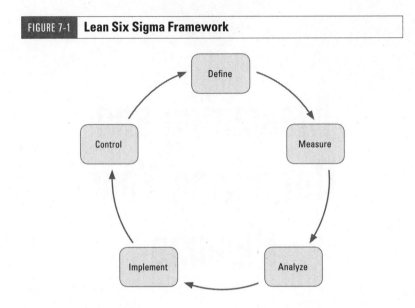

processes with the quality principles of six sigma. The second, Design Thinking, complements Lean Six Sigma by adding user centeredness and fast iteration. The steps in the two frameworks are shown in Figures 7-1 and 7-2.

The Define step in Lean Six Sigma corresponds to the Empathize/ Understand step in Design Thinking. In the context of Predictable Prospecting, Define means to articulate the part of the pipeline that needs to be optimized. Typical problems come from contacts getting stuck in a particular stage or wasting time by moving bad contacts to the next stage. Design Thinking asks sales managers and sales operations experts to empathize by taking a step back and putting themselves in the shoes of individual salespeople.

The Measure and Analyze steps in Lean Six Sigma link directly to the Observe/Research and Ideate/Brainstorm steps in Design Thinking. In both frameworks, the two steps are a combination of establishing starting point benchmarks for key

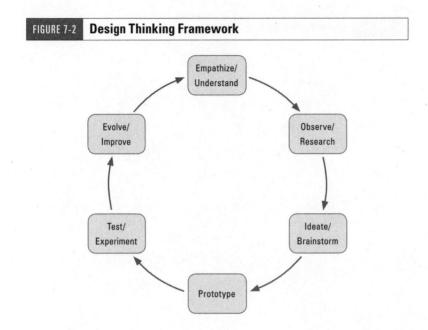

FIGURE 7-2   **Design Thinking Framework**

performance indicators (KPIs), developing hypotheses regarding the root causes of problems, and formulating viable and creative solutions. In any process, including Predictable Prospecting, these steps will reveal many opportunities. Hence, it is critical to spend time prioritizing the issues and opportunities based on business impact and degree of difficulty (see Figure 7-3). This issue prioritization classifies easy, high-impact issues as high; easy, low-impact and hard, high-impact issues as medium; and hard, low-impact issues as low.

The Implement step in Lean Six Sigma corresponds to two Design Thinking steps: Prototype and Test/Experiment. Here, one or more test solutions are designed and piloted.

Finally, the Control step in Lean Six Sigma links to the Evolve/ Improve step in Design Thinking. Assuming the results for the pilot were positive, the solution is scaled and the improvement cycle begins again.

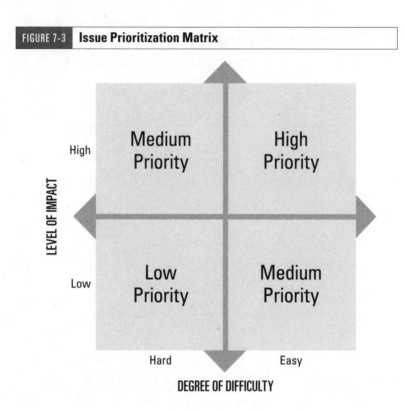

FIGURE 7-3   **Issue Prioritization Matrix**

The New Queue

Leads enter the New Queue from either inbound or outbound sources. Since some sources will turn out to be better than others, new leads should be tagged with a Lead Source attribute. Our rough ranking from highest to lowest quality of sources is as follows:

1. *Inbound:* Become a client

2. *Outbound:* Reactivation (of former clients)

3. *Outbound:* Referral

4. *Inbound:* Webinar

5. *Outbound:* Targeted lists assembled in-house

6. *Inbound:* White paper or e-book download

7. *Outbound:* Trade show lists

8. *Outbound:* Targeted lists sourced from third parties

Consider including a graph for volume by lead source. Sales leaders should monitor this graph to assess lead generation relative to targets or to inspect any service-level agreements established in partnership with their marketing department or agencies.

Note: For the inbound sources above, we have not distinguished how the leads were pulled in. For digital inbound leads, the main channels are direct, organic, or paid. Direct leads, where individuals enter a vendor's URL directly into their browser, are usually the best of the three. The other two are nearly of the same quality. Organic leads occur when an individual conducts a search and clicks on an unpaid link to a vendor's website. Investments in search engine optimization (SEO) increase the volume of organic leads by helping a company rank higher on the search engine results page (SERP). Paid leads occur when an individual clicks on an ad in a search engine, banner ad network, or social media property. In addition to these pay-per-click (PPC) leads, vendors can also pay third-party content publishers who host content on a per-lead basis.

When developing metrics for the New Queue, as well as other queues, we consider both intra-stage and inter-stage measures. Generally speaking, intra- (or within) stage measures include volume and cycle time. Inter- (or between) stage measures explore pipeline advancement or dropout and are usually expressed as percentages or ratios.

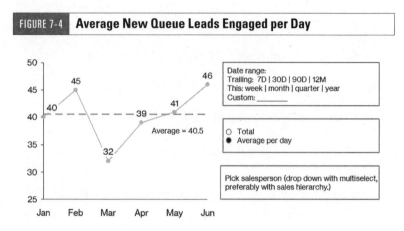

FIGURE 7-4   **Average New Queue Leads Engaged per Day**

In the charts that follow, we include six months of data for simplicity, but sales teams should choose the frequency that best suits their business. When possible, add one extra period to help identify deviations from normal seasonality—for example, five quarters of quarterly data or 13 months of monthly data.

As illustrated in Figure 7-4, the first New Queue measure to examine is the number of New Queue leads engaged (that is, those contacted for the first time). In this chart, we include the ability to toggle between the total number of leads engaged and the average number of leads engaged per day over a specific date range. The total comes in handy because quotas are often set over longer time horizons, typically monthly or quarterly. The average number of New Queue leads engaged per day is instrumental for coaching. When computing the average per day, only count business days worked in the denominator; though not perfect, the simplest way to make this adjustment is to include only days when an SDR engaged at least one lead.

Sales leaders should also examine the time it takes to engage New Queue leads as shown in Figure 7-5.

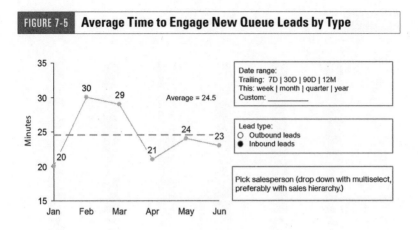

FIGURE 7-5   **Average Time to Engage New Queue Leads by Type**

Since leads from different sources are not created equal, the dashboard must include the ability to toggle between different types of leads. SDRs should respond within minutes to prospects who call in or submit contact forms seeking to speak with a salesperson. Inbound leads from content marketing can be responded to in hours or days; it can be unsettling for a prospect to receive a phone call mere minutes after downloading a white paper. Generally, outbound leads should be handled within days of being sourced. Based on performance to preestablished response time targets, different actions may be required:

1. If New Queue cycle time is increasing, the first option is always to improve the efficiency and productivity through process optimization, training, new technology, or job specialization.

2. If the team is efficient and sales are lagging behind targets, then the next option is adding sales capacity.

3. If the team is hitting targets and does not wish to add capacity, then the marketing team can scale back lead

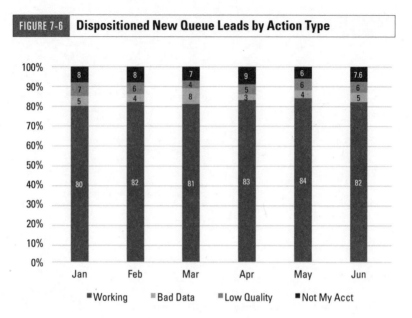

FIGURE 7-6   Dispositioned New Queue Leads by Action Type

generation either by engaging in less activity or, better yet, by improving lead quality by tightening up marketing-qualified lead (MQL) criteria.

Figure 7-6 shows New Queue lead disposition by type. Read this graph as follows: Of the new leads dispositioned in January, 80 percent were advanced to Working, a quality number that would probably be too low for most salespeople. Five percent were rejected for bad data, usually malformed contact information, obvious garbage (for example, Homer Simpson, Nuclear Safety Inspector, Springfield Nuclear Power Plant), or the contact was gone from the company. Seven percent were rejected for low quality, indicating either that the Ideal Prospect Profile needs to be updated or that leads are being put into the New Queue that do not adhere to the profile.

Many sales organizations are starting to look closely at the number of leads per account, represented as an average over

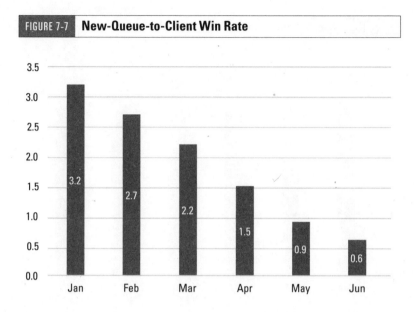

FIGURE 7-7 **New-Queue-to-Client Win Rate**

time, for at least two reasons. First, metrics from companies like the Corporate Executive Board show that an increasing number of individuals weigh in on B2B purchase decisions. Second, messaging multiple individuals at once in a personalized manner is a more strategic way to get around gatekeepers. If a salesperson does advance multiple contacts from the same company from the New Queue to the Working Queue, we recommend limiting the number to two or three at a time to avoid being flagged as a spammer. In addition, deliver a higher degree of personalization by referencing other people who were contacted.

Saving the best for last, we come to the most important New Queue metric. The ultimate measure of New Queue quality is whether or not new leads turn into paying customers, as illustrated in Figure 7-7. In the graph, 3.2 percent of new leads generated in January converted into paying customers. The downward ramp is as expected because leads need time to mature.

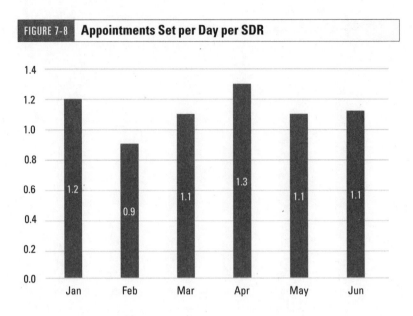

FIGURE 7-8   **Appointments Set per Day per SDR**

Many companies add a maximum duration cutoff so that the percentages are locked down at some point in time. Again, as with all other metrics, all values should be compared against targets.

The Working Queue

The most important Working Queue graph is the average number of appointments set per day per sales representative (see Figure 7-8). This graph is a fairly accurate representation of reality: most average outbound SDRs produce one appointment set per day while great ones can produce two or more. We also believe it is critical to track the appointment-set-to-appointment-held rate. In many organizations, SDRs (assuming they do not conduct first meetings) should only get credit for appointments held. Hence, if the prospect no-shows, the SDR remains on the hook

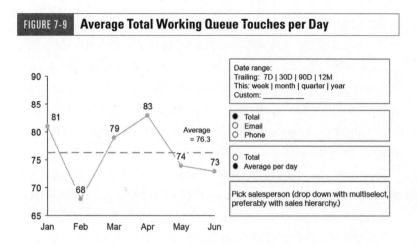

FIGURE 7-9 Average Total Working Queue Touches per Day

to reschedule the meeting. Leads are advanced to qualifying only *after* first meetings. Some SDRs will be better than others at ensuring prospects show up. Their best practices should be captured and shared.

Many activities drive the appointment set rate, beginning with touches per day (or touches per account per day). The two most common types of touches to track are e-mails and phone calls as illustrated in Figure 7-9. Additionally, some sales organizations track social media such as LinkedIn connects or Twitter direct message touches.

At a high level, one must understand how many touches in total are needed to secure an appointment; the most sophisticated sales teams optimize the touch cadence—the type, order, and frequency of touches. Additionally, sales leaders should track and optimize the meeting held rate (expressed as a percentage of the number of meetings set).

At the individual sales representative level, the most common e-mail metric tracked is the volume of e-mails sent per day per

SDR. More is not necessarily better because 50 truly customized e-mails may very well lead to more appointments than 100 mass-personalized e-mails. In terms of e-mail outcomes, the positive e-mail reply rate, typically around 3 percent, is the most important. For SDRs, there are several technologies that provide real-time notification when links are clicked, which is a great trigger to call a prospect to offer assistance.

Sales leaders tasked with optimization should look regularly at which e-mail templates are working best. Since it is difficult if not impossible to attribute meetings to any given touch, e-mail template effectiveness is often assessed by looking at the open rate and click-to-open rate (CTOR), or the click-through rate (CTR). The *open rate* is defined as the number of e-mails opened divided by the number of delivered e-mails. The benchmark for average open rate is 21 percent,[1] though open rates are becoming less and less reliable as e-mail clients do a better job of protecting user privacy. The *click-to-open rate* is defined as the number of unique clicks divided by the number of opens, and it averages 12.6 percent.[2] The *click-through rate* is the product of these other two, and it averages a paltry 2.6 percent. It is also wise to monitor unsubscribe rates and spam complaint rates to ensure that e-mails are not damaging relationships or your company's domain identity; benchmarks for these average 0.13 percent and 0.03 percent, respectively.

Next up are phone activity and outcome metrics. The most common are dials per day and talk time. We do not recommend setting either of these as primary objectives for SDRs (again, appointments are what matters). Setting a dials-per-day objective leads to reps feeling rushed to get off the phone. Setting a talk-time-per-day objective leads to reps leaving excessively long voice mails. We have even seen instances of reps calling weather services to hit these arbitrary numbers.

For phone activity, sales leaders often measure the dials-to-connect rate. When doing this, here are some benchmarks to consider:

- *Dials to connect:* It takes 12 direct-line dials to reach a prospect (8.3 percent connect rate).

- *Dials to conversation:* It takes 90 dials on average to secure an appointment (30 dials per conversation and 3 conversations per appointment).

- By dialing a direct line, reps are 46 percent more likely to reach a director and 147 percent more likely to reach a VP as compared to dialing through a switchboard. (*Bonus tip:* Be sure to ask the operator, "Can I have her number just in case we get disconnected?")[3]

For outcome activity, we prefer "meaningful conversation" as a measurement. A *meaningful conversation* is any conversation that furthers a prospect into (or out of) the sales pipeline. Consider the following metaphor. Driving along the freeway, you have exits and mile markers. Meaningful conversations that result in an unsuitable or not-yet-ready prospect falling out of the pipeline are exits. In contrast, meaningful conversations through which you learn more about a prospect show advancement and are mile markers. Conversations resulting in neither an exit nor a mile marker are not meaningful. Even more so than e-mails, phone calls, and meetings, the number of meaningful conversations needed to progress from one stage to the next is a critical metric.

Finally, sales leaders may wish to examine Working Queue cycle time. We do not consider this a primary dashboard metric like New Queue cycle time because we have not seen huge variations in SDR performance provided that each member of the team is maintaining appropriate activity levels.

The Qualifying and Closing Queues

After the first appointment is set and held, leads move on to the Qualifying Queue. The primary metric to follow is Qualifying Queue lead disposition by type (advanced to closing versus disqualified; recall that we do not recommend adding reporting complexity by requiring reps to choose a more detailed reason code for not qualified). Like Working Queue cycle time, Qualifying Queue cycle time by disposition type is a secondary metric.

Assuming the first appointment ends with an affirmative answer to the are-we-a-fit question, contacts become associated with opportunities and move into the Closing Queue. Here, we focus on similar metrics: first, Closing Queue lead disposition by type (transacted won or transacted lost) and second, Closing Queue cycle time. In addition, most organizations track metrics for opportunities by stage and also report on the weighted (or factored) pipeline to get a sense of revenue potential.

Case Study: SalesLoft

After stints as a bartender for a theater in Georgia, a manager for a youth hostel in Costa Rica, and a recruiter for a staffing organization, Sean Kester joined SalesLoft as its first sales development representative (SDR). SalesLoft competes in the sales workflow automation space with Outreach.io, PersistIQ, ToutApp, and Velocify. Over the years, Sean had risen to become the head of product, and his responsibilities included managing SalesLoft's entire SDR team. This meant he had to figuratively make and eat his own dog food. A self-described open book, Sean was kind enough to allow us to share a wealth of information. For starters, here is their first cold outreach e-mail template:

Subject Line: <First_Name>, SalesLoft + <Company>

<First_Name>,

<Highly_personalized_first_line>

I would like to learn about your outreach strategies at <Company>. We are working with other <industry> teams, helping their reps accelerate pipeline growth by 2 to 3 times.

To keep it simple, SalesLoft is a strategic platform that combines phone, e-mail, and social touches to ensure consistent execution of your sales cadence or outreach.

Don't take my word for it; you can try it yourself.

A brief screenshare on <two_business_days_from_now> or <three_business_days_from_now> would allow us to highlight how other teams are already streamlining their workflows as well as get you set up on a free trial. Which day would be better?

<Highly_personalized_last_line>

Next, here are SalesLoft's key metrics:

- On average, SDRs handle 700 to 800 outbound leads per month, or 35 to 40 per business day.

- 3.7 percent of net new outbound leads turn into a first (demo) meeting.

- On average, it takes six activities to secure a first meeting. Activities include e-mails, calls (with or without voice mail), LinkedIn views, Facebook likes, and Twitter follows.

- The average lead lifetime is 11.3 days, and 95 percent of outbound leads that convert do so in the first 30 days.

- 12.4 percent of inbound leads convert into a (demo) appointment.

- 95 percent of SalesLoft's pipeline is generated by SDRs.

Finally, here are several additional SalesLoft best practices:

- On the first day, SDRs first view the prospect's LinkedIn profile, and then they send an e-mail, and then call, leaving a voice mail if they do not connect.

- SDRs send *personalized* LinkedIn connections only *after* their first conversation with a prospect. (Do not merely send connections with LinkedIn's standard language that reads, "I'd like to add you to my professional network on LinkedIn.")

- SDRs spend less than 5 minutes personalizing the first and last line of each e-mail.

- To save time, SDRs drop voice mails (when they choose to do so) by leveraging one of five prerecorded templates.

- SalesLoft has found that sending LinkedIn Inmails referencing prospecting e-mails is an effective complement or alternative to leaving voice mails.

We urge sales professionals and sales leaders to adopt a "peel-the-onion" approach to optimization so as not to get overwhelmed by the many metrics presented in this chapter.

Start with the most important metrics: total sales relative to target and appointments held per rep per day. Set the target so that somewhere between 60 and 80 percent of SDRs hit the quota.

Next look at the New-Queue-to-customer win rate and interrogate the inter-stage conversation rates to detect any problem areas.

Then, go deeper into intra-stage metrics as needed. Also, while transparency is valuable, exposing people to highly volatile data is counterproductive, so be thoughtful about who should see what metrics at what frequency.

Finally, the measurement and optimization process requires a delicate balance between sales management who would like everything measured and sales professionals who see most activity tracking as a wasteful administrative burden. In Predictable Prospecting, we recommend the following two guidelines to help maintain this balance: First, sales training and sales force automation systems should be continuously aligned to best practices. Second, strive to eliminate the collection of any data that is either unlikely to be used or very likely to be garbage. It is for this reason that we do not recommend collecting reason codes for disqualification unless an organization is committed to using them.

Though execution, measurement, and optimization of Predictable Prospecting may seem daunting, there are many off-the-shelf tools and technologies designed to make tasks and processes simple so sales professionals can focus on activities that deliver deals. These sales productivity tools and technologies are the subject of our next chapter.

Leveraging the Right Tools

Since sales productivity tools come, go, and change so rapidly, we debated whether or not to include them, but, in the end, we decided to move forward by bringing their function to the foreground and relegating the form, the actual tools, to the background.

Sales tools must be viewed as a means to an end; they should support sales processes that help sales professionals close more deals at a faster rate. While that may seem obvious, nearly all salespeople have been saddled with tools that either slow them down or create barriers to building relationships with prospects. For instance, some tools allow salespeople to engage in less-than-ideal practices such as blasting impersonal e-mails to massive numbers of people. Therefore, we urge sales professionals to make conscious choices about the balance between automation and true personalization at each stage of the selling process.

Below, we outline capabilities aligned with stages of the Predictable Prospecting selling cycle.

Tools for the New Queue

By way of reminder, developing an Ideal Account Profile (IAP) is the first step in the Predictable Prospecting methodology. Where possible, an IAP should be based on one's best customers—the accounts with the highest lifetime value. At the account level, isolating desirable segmentation criteria, such as industry, size, and geography, is largely a manual task involving crafting and testing hypotheses. While there are statistical packages like SPSS and a growing ecosystem of predictive analytics vendors, most organizations still rely on traditional analysis tools such as Excel and Tableau. Once the IAP is defined, the most popular tool for *account identification* is Hoover's, although LinkedIn is rapidly gaining momentum. Additionally, upstarts such as InsideView and Unomy are also entering this relatively open segment.

With a set of target accounts aligned with an IAP, the next step is to build an Ideal Prospect Profile (IPP). Even more than building an IAP, constructing an IPP is a manual and highly qualitative exercise. The good news is that *contact discovery and management* tools abound for finding individuals aligned to the IPP. The highest-quality contact discovery tools are social networks, including LinkedIn and Facebook, where individuals maintain their own profiles. What's more, a supporting ecosystem of tools has cropped up to efficiently extract data from these sources.

Though a distant second, the next-most-accurate set of tools are those where contact information is manually verified; DiscoverOrg is a good example, at least for information technology contacts. Third in line are crowd-sourced contact databases such as Data.com, ZoomInfo, and CircleBack. Especially with a crowd-sourced contact database, test rigorously before you buy because they are infamous for low data quality. A forth option are web scrapers, the most popular of which is currently eGrabber. In addition, once a contact is identified, a salesperson can manage and stay engaged by using a variety of tools, including Accompany, CharlieApp, Contactually, Discover.ly, Found.ly, InsideView, LinkedIn, and Nimble.

Now, we move on to *sales enablement* tools for selecting the right content to use with prospects at the right time. Providers in this space include Act-on software, Bloomfire, CallidusCloud Enablement, DecisionLink, Docurated, KnowledgeTree, Microsoft SharePoint, MindMatrix, Playboox, Qvidian, Seismic, and Skura.

Once a contact database gets even moderately large, it can be extremely difficult to prioritize the right prospects to engage. To solve that problem, a new generation of *predictive analytics* companies has emerged, including 6Sense, Fliptop, Infer, Lattice Engines, Mintigo, and SalesPredict. Predictive analytics uses machine learning to build and dynamically evolve both ideal account and ideal prospect profiles. Specifically, this software combines internal data such as win and loss information with external data on contacts and accounts to score inbound and outbound leads and to highlight upsell opportunities and retention risks with existing clients.

Though we have focused mainly on tools to build the outbound New Queue, it is, on average, easier to engage an inbound lead than to (re-)activate a nurtured lead. This brings us into the world of *marketing automation platforms* (MAPs) such as Adobe Marketing Cloud, Eloqua, HubSpot, Infusionsoft, Marketo, Pardot, and SalesFusion. Traditional MAPs push content (usually via e-mail) and send leads to salespeople once engagement reaches a certain level. Next generation MAPs, styled as 'virtual assistants powered by artificial intelligence,' can hold electronic dialogue. For instance, Brent Holloway, VP of Corporate Sales at Talend, uses Conversica to reach out to leads with low scores that his sales team would not otherwise have the capacity to engage.

Tools for the Working Queue

In Predictable Prospecting, the Working Queue starts with the first attempt to contact a prospect and ends either when an are-we-a-fit (AWAF) meeting is held or when an unresponsive lead is moved to nurturing. Though managing overlapping multitouch campaigns through brute force is (barely) possible, many sales organizations are turning to *sales workflow automation* tools, including Outreach.io, PersistIQ, SalesLoft Cadence, ToutApp, and Velocify. Most of these tools have integrated phone dialers, but other options are available, including front-runner InsideSales.com and newcomer Five9.

Likewise, most of the sales workflow automation tools have the ability to send e-mail as well as to track opens, clicks, and replies. Even if one does not use a sales workflow automation tool, there are many *e-mail activity tracking* tools available such as SideKick (formerly known as Signals), Tellwise, and Yesware. For mass e-mailing, something we do not recommend unless prospects have opted in, there are many *e-mail marketing* services, including Silverpop and MailChimp. In addition, there are even *e-mail discovery* tools that allow salespeople to find e-mails with using only, say, first name, last name, and domain and not having to guess at various combinations. These include Discover.ly, eGrabber, e-mail-format.com, Rapportive, and Toofr. Finally, to save the hassle of going back and forth via e-mail to pick meeting times, *meeting scheduling* tools like Assistant.to and Calendly are currently popular time-savers.

E-mail quality tools are quick and easy utilities for avoiding spam filters. Many people are not even aware they exist. Just search for "e-mail spam checker" to find countless free, online resources. With some, like mail-tester.com, you can simply send your e-mail to an address for analysis. With others, such as e-mailspamtest.com, http://lyris.com/us-en/contentchecker, or http://info.contactology.com/check-mqs, you can just enter information into a form, and you will get an immediate response. This functionality is also built into many e-mail marketing services (such as those mentioned above).

We are on the fence about whether or not to recommend *e-mail verification services* like Fresh Address, verify-e-mail.org, e-mail-checker.net, BriteVerify, and Kickbox.io. These services connect with a mail server, transmit a from/to address pair, receive an acknowledgement, and then disconnect before actually sending an e-mail. Most often, the acknowledgement status is either accept, reject, or accept all. Accept, as one would imagine, means the mail server verified the address as valid. However, many companies post "valid" dummy e-mail addresses online as bait to catch spammers so even an accept status is not golden. The reject acknowledgement can be trusted, and those e-mails should be removed from one's database. And "accept all" means that a mail server, well, accepts every e-mail as valid, which the server does to protect employees from spammers. If a server set to accept all receives too much undeliverable mail, then the sender's domain will likely end up on an e-mail blacklist. These blacklists are usually shared by many mail servers, and getting removed from any of them can be complex and expensive. No salesperson wants to be the one that got her company's domain blacklisted. We conducted a small test using one of the services and found 25 percent were accepted, 12 percent were rejected, and the remaining 63 percent were accept all. At the very least, we were able to remove the rejected e-mails from our database.

Contact research tools round out the group of Working Queue resources. They accelerate precedence planning by assembling disparate digital information about contacts in a single view. While some of these are standalone, many integrate with e-mail and CRM systems, mostly Gmail and Salesforce.com, respectively. Three of the many options currently available include InsideView, Owler, and Vibe.

Tools for the Qualifying Queue

The Qualifying Queue has a very short cycle time, ranging from the time a salesperson completes the initial AWAF call to accepting a lead into the closing pipeline. During the AWAF call, many sales professionals deliver at least a few slides of their pitch deck or share their desktop. The *web conferencing* category is mature with many vendors, including Citrix GoToMeeting, Cisco Webex, ClearSlide, and Join.Me. For salespeople who choose to send collateral and want to verify prospect engagement, there are *document tracking* tools such as Attach, Clearslide, and DocSend.

Tools for the Closing and Servicing Queue

Since this book is mainly about prospecting new leads through qualifying, we offer only two categories of innovative tools for closing and servicing. In the closing category, *digital contract management* tools such as Callidus CLM, DocuSign, and EchoSign have become very popular. In the servicing category, particularly for recurring revenue services, GainSight and Salesforce.com's service cloud are both quality options.

This chapter was written under the assumption that sales professionals have little discretion in choosing their overarching CRM system, so we didn't go down that road. Likewise, we have avoided business intelligence and reporting tools (of which there are many besides Domo, Qlik, and Tableau). We also skipped the emerging class of mobile-enabled, video-rich, often-gamified sales training tools; however, two we have run across that are sales specific are CommercialTribe and Qstream.

CHAPTER

9

Managing Sales Development Professionals

Every successful manager, whether in sales or elsewhere, must possess a mix of strategic, operational, and leadership skills. However, the mix of required skills varies greatly as a function of the team's objectives. Consider the differences between traditional sales managers (TSMs) and business development managers (BDMs). TSMs hold individuals accountable to monthly or quarterly goals while BDMs must be on top of daily activity. TSMs optimize and coach for success on farming while BDMs focus on hunting. TSMs tend to manage more experienced professionals than do BDMs. All of this means that TSMs tend to be more balanced across strategic, operational, and people leadership. BSMs, on the other hand, should be overweighted on operational excellence and people development.

Insource Sales Development

Before we go any further, a critical issue that we need to address concerns whether an organization should insource or outsource the sales development function, particularly if sales development is geared toward appointment setting. We urge sales leaders to insource sales development. Sure, outsourcing has certain advantages in that outsourcers offer flexible capacity and are usually well outfitted with the latest tools and technology including dialers and campaign automation. Also, outsourcers, at least in theory, are well along the experience curve in terms of templates and best practices. The world of B2B sales development has evolved from spray-and-pray numbers games to highly personalized, account-based selling, making the benefits of outsourcing not worth the costs.

Let's start with the price one pays for flexible capacity. It is not the *flex* part of *flexible* that we have an issue with. It is the *(a)ble* part. Depending on the complexity of an organization's products and services, it can take 3, 6, 9, 12, or more months to adequately train a sales development professional. The Bridge Group found that the average ramp to full productivity is 3.8 months, though there is wide variation as shown in Figure 9-1.[1] Technology and sales process skills are the least of it. Customer, product, and competitor knowledge are the most important aspects of training. Moreover, outsourcing sales development removes an incredibly valuable talent pipeline of future account executives.

Next, consider tools and technology. Years ago, appointment setting outsourcers had a major advantage in being able to spread the costs of telephony systems and enterprise software licenses and support across many customers. But this advantage has been neutralized with the advent of high-quality Internet telephony

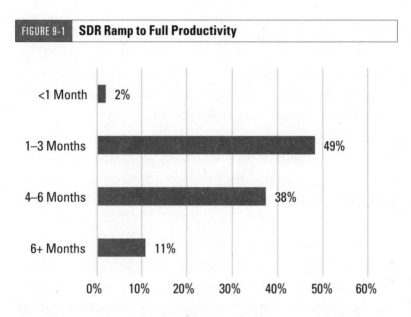

FIGURE 9-1   SDR Ramp to Full Productivity

<1 Month 2%

1–3 Months 49%

4–6 Months 38%

6+ Months 11%

0%   10%   20%   30%   40%   50%   60%

Source: Trish Bertuzzi, *Sales Development Rep (SDR) 2014 Metrics and Compensation*, Bridge Group, Inc., Hudson, MA, 2014.

and cloud-based (aka software-as-a-service, or SaaS) platforms. Most tools can be purchased on a per-user, month-to-month basis. Additionally, many organizations were either not able to or did not want to connect an outsourcer's platform with the company's customer relationship management system. Today's cloud-based tools make that easy. With average technical proficiency, we've seen teams integrate and configure these tools within days.

Last, with respect to the insourcing/outsourcing decision, we turn to best practices and templates. Again, years ago, outsourcers had a major advantage. But two neutralizing forces have leveled the playing field. One, competition for organic search traffic has led to an explosion in content marketing. Companies competing in and around marketing and sales automation publish data-driven studies and share best practices by the truckload. Two, the shift from spray-and-pray to account-based selling has made generic templates less valuable. When every e-mail sent and every voice mail dropped requires personalization, generic templates are more harmful than helpful.

We racked our brains to think of exceptions where we would actually recommend outsourcing. It took some time, but we eventually came up with one: the solopreneur. We know consultants who are very happy running their one-person shops and do not aspire to scale up. Many are time limited rather than opportunity limited. Consequently, these individuals need only a partial business development resource to set enough appointments to maintain a small backlog, making them the exception to the rule. Everyone else should insource sales business development, including appointment setting.

Attract a Strong Pool of Candidates

Conventional wisdom suggests that employee referral programs are the best source of talent. When "best" is measured on three factors—recruiting cost, employee tenure, and job performance—the conventional wisdom gets it right on two out of the three.

First, examining hiring at a manufacturing plant of a Fortune 500 high-tech organization, academic researchers from Technion Institute of Technology confirmed that the recruiting cost from employee referrals was significantly better (lower) than from other sources.[2] Out of 1,545 applicants, the organization in the study spent $521,000 to hire 131 employees; hence, the average cost per new hire was $627. While that average cost may seem low, the recruiting source varied wildly, as can be seen below (*note*: the yield—the percentage of applicants hired—is shown in parentheses):

- National newspaper advertising: $81,000 (1.8 percent)

- Local newspaper advertising: $1,149 (7.3 percent)

- Employee referral: $0 (13.3 percent)

In this study, the superiority of employee referrals can be attributed to the low yield of newspaper advertising as well as to the fact that the company did not have a paid employee referral program in place. Unfortunately, the researchers excluded two other interesting sources: self-initiated walk-ins and employment agencies.

Second, researchers from Radford University confirmed that referral employees have a longer tenure by combining the results of 11 studies.[3] They found the following differences between recruitment sources and tenure: (1) employee referral hires stay 20 percent longer than average, (2) direct application hires stay 1 percent shorter than average, (3) employment agency hires stay 8 percent shorter than average, and (4) media advertisement hires stay 11 percent shorter than average.

Third, the conventional belief that referred employees are better performers has not been confirmed conclusively by academic research. Most studies, including the Radford University meta-analysis just cited, show that performance on the job is independent of recruiting source.

In summary, these studies confirm hiring via referral is best. While performance is ultimately unrelated to hiring source, referred employees are cheaper to hire and they tend to stay longer.

Regardless of the hiring source, employers seeking to attract sales development representatives must craft compelling job descriptions. The best job descriptions contain the following elements:

- Language that gives candidates the sense that your organization is a great place to learn and advance their careers

  Example: We are seeking candidates looking to advance their careers by joining our sales development team in Salt Lake City, Utah. We are committed to investing in your future by training you in sales and professional skills that will serve you here at (company name) or beyond. Depending on performance, our sales development professionals are promoted to account executive after 18 months.

- A simple explanation of day-to-day duties

  Example: You will be responsible for supporting the sales efforts of your team, including sourcing, establishing, and building relationships with corporate executives over the phone and by e-mail. You will be responsible for researching and identifying new client opportunities, presenting our services to prospects and clients to increase awareness of our brand, using our CRM system to track and map client accounts, and working to drive adoption and usage of our services.

- Jargon-free attributes of top performers separated by strict requirements and nice-to-haves

  Example: An ideal candidate must have the following:
  - A bachelor's degree with a GPA exceeding 3.3 out of 4.0
  - Superior verbal and written communication skills
  - Comfort with high-activity phone and e-mail prospecting
  - Keen attention to detail and motivation to deliver high-quality work product
  - Ability to build strong and lasting relationships with key decision makers in client firms

- Ability to work well independently and be self-motivated as well as work on a team and across functional areas of an organization

An ideal candidate should have the following:
- 1 to 4 years of relevant work experience in sales development and/or the manufacturing industry
- Overview of your organization and its core values

Example: (Company name) is the world's leading platform for (service). Business leaders, investors, consultants, social entrepreneurs, and other top professionals rely on (company name) to (primary benefit). Clients partner with (company name) to take advantage of (primary features). We believe strongly in our mission- and values-driven culture. Our core values drive our success. They are: (values).

We placed learning and advancement first on the list because candidates for SDR positions ask us most frequently about those topics. Learning should include functional sales skills as well as general professional skills. Advancement means clarity on the promotion path. With respect to the latter, sales guru Trish Bertuzzi recommends establishing micropromotions. For instance, in a one-year program, a new hire might graduate from an associate SDR who sets appointments to a senior SDR who generates qualified opportunities. Such promotions must be based on achievement, not on tenure.

Last, we usually avoid including salary range in the job description. Instead, we ask for the expected salary range when candidates apply so that we can weed out candidates whose expectations are too high. In our own experience, we would rather not fall in love with an expensive candidate because it wastes everyone's time and such candidates artificially and unfairly raise the bar on the realistic candidate pool. In the end, hire the best candidate given the money you budgeted. Quickly release the ones who don't perform, and extravagantly reward the ones who do with recognition and compensation.

Hire and Train Smart, Conscientious, Articulate, Early-Career Individuals

Every sales leader knows that hiring skill is critical to success. According to *CSO Insights*,[4] overall sales representative turnover averages 22.4 percent, half of which is voluntary. In our experience, turnover is even higher among sales development teams where the employees are often younger and the work is both routine and stressful and managers must "always be hiring" to get ahead of inevitable attrition.

The ideal sales development new hire is a highly successful hunter working for a competitor who comes in via referral from an internal star performer. Of course, such a rare individual is not making a move anywhere unless offered a massive increase in pay and responsibility. Unfortunately, the job of a sales development professional is typically entry level and, therefore, commands neither high compensation nor a broad span of control.

So whom should you hire? Fortunately, academic researchers have spent years searching for the answer to just this question, and they have come to some amazingly valuable conclusions. Shockingly, very few hiring managers are aware of these findings, and among those who are, few apply them. We are willing to bet that *the* major deciding factor when you were last hired (or when you last hired someone) was an informal, face-to-face interview. Well, Frank Schmidt from the University of Iowa and John E. Hunter from Michigan State University proved more than a decade ago that that is a terrible way to hire.[5] General mental ability (GMA) is the best predictor of hiring success, accounting for 26 percent of the variation in job performance. Adding an unstructured interview to an intelligence test increases the explanation of performance variation by a mere four points to 30 percent. Administering IQ tests, something almost nobody does, is way better than conducting informal interviews. On their own, unstructured interviews predict only 14 percent of variation in job performance.

Two other tests, a work sample test and a test of conscientiousness, are also better than informal interviews. While each takes more effort to conduct, work sample tests and hands-on job simulations add 13 points to the explanation of variation in job performance. Conscientiousness tests add 10 points. Though Schmidt and Hunter's meta-analysis considered many types of jobs, other researchers found similar predictors of sales performance. A group of professors from the University of Iowa showed that "sales representatives high in conscientiousness are more likely to set goals and are more likely to be committed to goals, which in turn is associated with greater sales volume and higher supervisory ratings of job performance."[6] Moreover, in contrast to conventional wisdom, these same researchers found extraversion is *not related* to either sales volume or supervisory ratings of job performance.

A trio of researchers from Erasmus University, Rotterdam, added the missing piece. In addition to GMA (characterized as cognitive aptitude) and conscientiousness (characterized as the degree of adaptiveness and the ability to deal with role ambiguity), their study[7] found selling-related knowledge to be a statistically significant driver of sales performance. They defined *selling-related knowledge* as that which "reflects the knowledge of both products and customers that is required to present and 'co-create' solutions for customers."

Let's pull all of this together. Experienced account executives create more economic value in senior account management roles. Moreover, an experienced account executive might not accept the monotony and relatively low degree of control even with adequate pay. Hence, in most circumstances, organizations will be able to hire only early-career professionals into sales development roles. A successful evaluation of candidates can be made using (a) a GMA test or rigorous screening based on past academic performance, (b) a test of conscientiousness, (c) a test of sales aptitude, and (d) a structured role-play to assess many factors including selling skill and communication ability.

We have investigated a number of commercial tests of sales aptitude including those from Devine/Sandler, Objective Management Group (OMG), Predictive Index (PI), SalesGenomix, and Talent Analytics. We prefer tests composed of forced-choice questions. This means candidates must choose the better of two desirable options or the lesser of two evils. For instance, "Would you describe yourself as more intelligent or more conscientious?" or "Would you rather miss your quota while your team makes theirs or make your quota while your team misses theirs?"

The Devine/Sandler and Talent Analytics tests are two of our favorites in this category. The Devine/Sandler test conveniently provides scores relative to benchmarks the vendor has developed by sales role. The Talent Analytics assessment requires that you develop your own benchmark by first applying the survey instruments to your organization's top performers. In our eyes, this makes Devine/Sandler better for smaller organizations and Talent Analytics better for larger ones. Either way, you should test at least two of the assessments to identify which is better able to identify individuals likely to become top performers in your organization.

Here is how we use assessments: First, stack rank your existing sales organization using fact-based metrics such as performance-to-quota, new business generated (for hunters), or uncapped wallet retention (for farmers). Second, carefully review the stack rank to make sure it is accurate; adjust or remove any glaring anomalies that have special circumstances such as an account manager who lost a major account due to an external factor like bankruptcy. However, do not make adjustments based on managers' opinions. Third, assess the top and bottom quartiles and develop a set of attribute weights that maximizes the score difference between the two populations. Fourth, verify that the resulting model is non-discriminatory. For new job candidates who score in the top quartile, move quickly to hire while looking for red flags. For new job candidates who score in the middle 50 percent, the assessment provides little information. Last, eliminate new job candidates who score in the bottom quartile from the hiring process *unless* there is something otherwise exceptional about them. Personality-based assessments should be only one of many factors used in hiring.

As for the role-play, we recommend a test we affectionately call the Kobayashi Maru. (*Star Trek* aficionados will recognize this as the no-win test of character command-track cadets must endure to graduate from Starfleet Academy.) In this test, we ask candidates to call us and try to schedule an appointment for our product. We relentlessly throw objection after objection at them: "Send me some information," "I need to run to a meeting," "I don't see the ROI," "I don't understand what you are saying," and so on. We do not yet care about their product knowledge. Instead, we judge two factors: The most important is their ability to persevere through at least three objections. The second is the degree to which they remain articulate throughout the process.

Where possible, hire individuals with some experience, either in a B2B sales role or in the industry an organization sells into. Seek out more experience (and expect to pay more) when selling

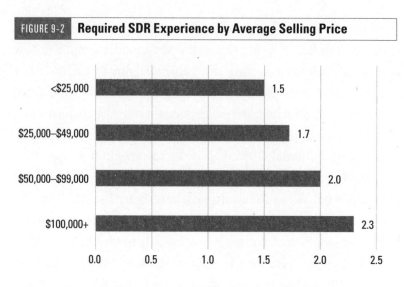

FIGURE 9-2 **Required SDR Experience by Average Selling Price**

Source: Trish Bertuzzi, *Sales Development Rep (SDR) 2014 Metrics and Compensation*, Bridge Group, Inc., Hudson, MA, 2014.

a high-priced, complex product or service to very senior executives. The Bridge Group found required experience for sales development representatives selling $25,000 to $50,000 solutions averaged 1.7 years, while those selling $100,000+ solutions averaged 2.3 years (see Figure 9-2). Then, systematically train new sales development hires separately from seasoned account executives in a combination of customer knowledge, value messaging, product knowledge, competitive knowledge, sales skills and behaviors (verbal communication, business writing, objection handling), best-practice processes, and technology platforms.

With respect to hiring, we recommend bringing on sales development representatives in cohorts rather than one at a time. As Craig Ferrara, vice president of client operations for AG Salesworks, noted,[8] benefits include strong peer learning, accurate benchmarking, productive competition, efficient training, and lower risk to sales volatility.

SDRs, typically early-career sales professionals, expect and deserve extensive training. The best organizations hold weekly team meetings focused on training. Some organizations even train on a daily basis. In addition, best-in-class organizations test their SDRs and recognize success with extrinsic (money) and intrinsic (certificates, experiences) rewards. As mentioned previously, training should focus on a range of areas such as technology, sales skills, soft skills, products, accounts, and competitors. SDR leaders should maintain and share a sales development playbook that includes ideal account and prospect profiles, qualification criteria, multitouch cadences, voice mail talking points, objection handling guidance, e-mail templates, technology tutorials, hiring criteria, and career paths.

Though most training occurs on the job, team and one-on-one training can be especially effective. In team sessions, we emphasize role-paying, analyzing sales e-mails sent by other companies, interviewing friendly customers, reviewing books, and listening to call recordings. In one-on-ones, managers should review activity and results as well as call recordings. One SDR leader we spoke with requires his SDRs to bring their best call and worst call to their one-on-ones. The best calls are scored using an objective scorecard and go into a shared "Hall of Fame" repository.

Hire Dedicated Sales Development Managers

Leaders face an array of organizational structure decisions, especially when starting a new development function, the first being whether it should roll into the sales or the marketing organization. Unfortunately, we have not been able to find any studies comparing the performance of sales development groups reporting to one function or the other. Our sense is that the top-level reporting structure is irrelevant compared to other factors such as hiring, the first-line manager, or process optimization. Organizations that are highly dependent on inbound leads tend to roll sales development into marketing to ensure the immediacy of response and consistency of message. In contrast, organizations that are highly dependent upon outbound prospecting tend to roll the function into sales to ensure that the right accounts and contacts are prioritized.

Fortunately, thanks to The Bridge Group,[9] we can at least share that most companies, 73 percent in fact, place sales development within the sales organization. Of the remainder, 24 percent roll the function into marketing, and 3 percent locate it elsewhere. We agree with Trish Bertuzzi of The Bridge Group, who recommends, "This team reports to whoever has the expertise, passion, and bandwidth to lead it. This is far more important than what 'everybody else' is doing." In almost all circumstances, we recommend that organizations recruit sales development managers from *within* the company because their people need leaders who know the products, prospects, and process inside and out.

To that end, start by looking within the sales development organization for talent. However, beware of simply promoting the top performing SDR to manager. Often, high performers are ruthlessly independent. Instead, look for an above average performer whom other SDRs trust and go to for answers. While we prefer pure managers to player-coaches, we recommend that SDR managers run a short cadence with a small number of prospects at least once a quarter to stay in tune with what is working and what is not, as well as to earn credibility with their team (even if the manager is unsuccessful in booking meetings or qualifying opportunities).

Assuming one follows the majority, the next decision is whether to centralize or decentralize the sales development function. Outbound sales development professionals should be aligned with but not report to individual sales managers. Traditional B2B sales managers typically lead six to eight account executives (AEs). Since the industry average is one SDR for every four AEs,[10] an average sales team could be supported by one or two SDRs. Hence, SDR territory strategy will naturally mirror AE territory strategy.

Alignment does not imply reporting structure. We strongly recommend centralizing the sales development function by having dedicated sales development managers, each with a span of control of six to eight SDRs. Since new hires need to respect and learn from their manager, we *insist* the team manager come from inside the company with success as a hunter and possess an analytical mindset as well as solid selling skills knowledge.

Turning to the next organizational structure decision, geographic placement, we recommend collocating the new team in an office with a concentration of experienced account executives when starting a sales development function. This is especially important early on, when the account executives must share feedback about practices that have worked and not worked for them. Our philosophy in piloting new initiatives is to "stack the deck." This means removing any factors that might later be used as an excuse to explain failure. If a pilot fails under the best conditions, then one knows the initiative will not work at scale. After proving success, a scaled-up sales development function can be located in a lower-cost long-term location with a sizable, well-educated talent pool. In the United States, great locations include Salt Lake City, Austin, and Raleigh-Durham.

The final organizational structure decision concerns whether to combine or separate inbound and outbound sales development. Figure 9-3 shows a little more than half, 55 percent, of organizations adopt a blended approach.

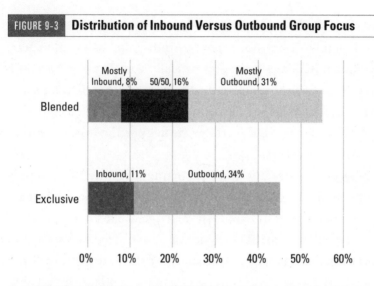

FIGURE 9-3   Distribution of Inbound Versus Outbound Group Focus

Source: Trish Bertuzzi, *Sales Development Rep (SDR) 2014 Metrics and Compensation*, Bridge Group, Inc., Hudson, MA, 2014.

We believe there is little consistency in combining or separating inbound and outbound sales development because the decision is extremely context dependent. Though rapid response to inbound leads is critical, the decision depends on several factors, including these:

- *The volume of inbound leads:* The lower the volume, the more likely the sales development focus will be blended.

- *The breadth of customer needs:* The more diverse the customer base, the more likely the sales development focus will be blended because SDRs need domain expertise to connect on a meaningful level with prospects.

- *The breadth of the product portfolio:* The broader the product portfolio, the more likely sales development will be blended.

Enable Sales Development Professionals with Process and Technology

As we explored in detail in the previous chapter, sales development professionals should have access to tools that either allow them to do things they would otherwise not be able to do (run overlapping multitouch, multichannel campaigns) or streamline routine work (dial at the click of a button and record activity in their CRM). In addition, SDRs should have access to a campaign library consisting of proven contact frequency and duration cadences, e-mail templates, voice mail scripts, and compelling content and collateral.

In smaller sales development teams, SDRs will likely be responsible for gathering their own leads from a variety of data sources. As a team grows, it pays to separate outbound lead acquisition into its own function. High-quality data is paramount to sales effectiveness, so investments in cleaning contact information pay huge dividends. Organizations that adopt this level of specialization must build robust contact validation processes because low-quality leads waste time and lower motivation.

Reward Results, Not Activity

Consider for a moment all of the data points generated by sales development professionals as their prospects move from the top to the bottom of the funnel: new contacts added, e-mails, phone calls (dials, connects, voice mails, talk time), appointments set, appointments completed, leads accepted (and linked to opportunities), and, finally, closed-won business. Common benchmarks are 50 dials and 8 connects per day; 1 appointment set per day; and 8 opportunities added per month. The Bridge Group, whom we have cited with permission many times thus far, identified over 30 different variable compensation schemes in their survey. While most organizations use only one or two factors, 28 percent apply three or more components to calculate incentive pay.[11] In doing so, they violate *the* core tenet of compensation design: simplicity.

While we find it useful to monitor top-of-funnel activity including dials and e-mails, we strongly recommend against elevating their stature. When those metrics become either widely syndicated or included in compensation plans, bad things start to happen. To achieve their dial numbers, SDRs may cut short what might otherwise be valuable conversations. To achieve their e-mail numbers, SDRs may underpersonalize their messages, which then come across as "spammy." We support call monitoring and (where legal) call recording for constructive coaching purposes but not for punishment.

Similarly, we find it critically valuable to monitor the ultimate bottom-of-the-funnel metric, revenue from closed-won business. What percent of total company revenue is typically sourced by SDRs? According to The Bridge Group's study, 45 percent. However, unlike dials and e-mails, where SDRs have too much control, closed-won business is a metric over which SDRs have too little control. Compensation should never be tied to factors over which employees have little or no control. This said, we support the common practice of awarding SDRs a special bonus of up to 1 percent on transacted business they were involved with; this level is subtly motivating without being distracting.

The right place to find metrics for SDR incentive compensation is right in the middle of the funnel. A recent survey[12] found 65 percent of sales development groups are focused on generating qualified opportunities, 26 percent on appointment setting, and 9 percent on a combination of the two. For teams that generate qualified opportunities, we believe the single metric to use for variable compensation is opportunities *accepted* by account executive.

We prefer accepted rather than generated because it adds an important layer of quality control. If account executives are inspected on the close rate of opportunities in their pipeline, they will not accept junk just to help out their SDR partners. For teams that set appointments, we believe the single metric to use for variable compensation is leads accepted. Appointments set is not a strong enough metric since the SDR's job is not done until the appointment is held.

Moreover, appointments held is not a strong enough metric either because, as with opportunities accepted, there needs to be some degree of quality control. We are willing to live with the fact that account executives might overaccept leads from appointment-setting professionals since it would not be fair to compensate SDRs on qualified opportunities—their doing so is too dependent on the skill of the account executive.

With all this talk of incentive compensation, we would be remiss if we did not suggest paying SDRs a base salary alone. This strategy is particularly effective with good management and measurement combined with an expectation that SDRs move up or out after 12 months. Often, vying for a promotion or seeing one's position on a leaderboard is incentive enough to drive high performance.

Our final piece of advice on managing sales development professionals is to remember to treat SDRs as human beings. This was our guiding principle when writing this chapter. Compensating SDRs on midfunnel results rather than top-of-funnel activity empowers them to do what is right for prospects and for the organization. If most associates reach out to 50 prospects per day to get one appointment and one associate accomplishes the same goal reaching out to only 10 prospects, then so be it. Countless studies[13] have proven that job satisfaction is closely linked to control. Since highly optimized sales development processes take away a decent amount of individuality, managers must strive to find ways to give back as much autonomy as possible to SDRs.

Let's also not forget that much of the glory among sales teams goes to rainmakers, the seasoned account executives who bring in the most sales. We believe SDRs need to be viewed as full members of the sales team and celebrated equally for their contributions.

Twelve Habits of Highly Successful SDRs

As a result of the many books the two of us have read on selling, we have come to the conclusion that there is little new under the sun concerning the habits of highly successful salespeople. However, that doesn't mean we don't appreciate a reminder now and again to revisit what we do know, should do, and don't always practice. Our guidance falls into three broad categories: time management, communication, and professional effectiveness.

Time Management

1. Focus

Focus operates at both the macro- and the microlevels. At the macrolevel, focus is about setting **s**pecific, **m**easurable, **a**chievable and/or attainable, **r**ealistic and/or relevant, and **t**ime-bound (SMART) goals. At the microlevel, focus is about removing distractions in order to concentrate on results-driven activities.

In our experience, people struggle more with microlevel focus than they do with macrolevel focus. This mirrors the well-known social science finding that average people rate themselves as above average, and based on our observations, most people are under the assumption that they multitask well while others do not. This type of thinking is especially common among millennials who argue that they were raised in a multitasking environment and are therefore better at it. We haven't seen that to be the case, and many rigorous academic studies have not only backed that up but have dispelled that myth. Consider a recent study of 145 college students recruited from a second-year research methods and statistics course.[1] Although all of the students attended a sequence of three lectures together, the researchers assigned each student to one of seven groups as follows: (1) paper-and-pencil note-taking only, (2) word processing note-taking only, (3) natural use of technology (that is, the control group in which participants were allowed to use technology as they normally would during lectures), (4) multitasking on Facebook, (5) multitasking on e-mail, (6) multitasking on MSN Instant Messenger, and (7) multitasking on a texting application. The average scores across three 15-question multiple-choice tests, each conducted following a lecture, are provided in Figure 10-1.

The results suggested that immersive social networking and e-mailing lead to cognitive impairment, even in millennials. Salespeople, be they millennials or not, are prone to all of these same distractions. To conquer this, we turn to the next habit, schedule.

2. Schedule

Distractions are contextual—e-mail qualifies as a distraction only when you are supposed to be doing something else. To maximize productivity, we recommend that sales professionals batch

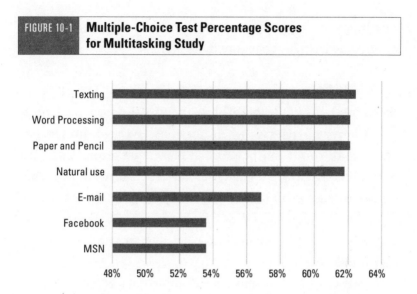

FIGURE 10-1 | **Multiple-Choice Test Percentage Scores for Multitasking Study**

tasks into time blocks scheduled on their calendars. Aaron Ross's sage advice in the foreword of this book is that prospecting must be done in blocks lasting a minimum of two hours. This means that prospecting activity blocks need to be scheduled for the most productive time of each day (that usually means first thing in the morning) so that this behavior becomes a habit.

Moreover, stay on task religiously either through force of will or with digital distraction-blocking technologies such as Freedom or Anti-Social. If you have not already done so, turn off all but the most critical notifications on your phone and computing devices.

3. Plan

Trim often unwieldy longer-term goals into shorter, smaller, more manageable pieces, and make it easier to measure success. It's not uncommon for many sales development representatives to have a goal of setting 20 qualified appointments per month, but break this down into a weekly goal of 5 appointments, or, even better, a daily goal of 1 appointment, and you'll actually see success on an ongoing basis and be more motivated.

4. Delegate

To maintain (the illusion of) total control, salespeople tend to underdelegate. Instead, when possible, leverage the services available to you from the product team, marketing, and sales operations. Even when you don't have such services available, virtual assistants can take care of many administrative tasks.

We are big fans of David Allen's book *Getting Things Done,* and we have slightly adapted his efficient framework for delegation as follows.

First, delegate a task only when completing it will not help you achieve your focus goals.

Second, delegate an important task only when you are not uniquely qualified to complete it yourself.

Third, don't delegate an important task if you are uniquely qualified to complete it in a trivial amount of time, usually not more than five minutes.

Fourth, schedule a task on your calendar only if you expect it to take a meaningful length of time to complete.

Communication

5. Smile

We would have loved to provide support for the facial-feedback hypothesis, which posits, according to none other than Charles Darwin and William James, that the mere act of smiling can cause happiness, but research[2] has failed to confirm it. Instead, it has been proven that highly authentic emotional displays by employees "can trigger changes in a customer's affective state."

Specifically, "the authenticity of the employee's emotional labor display, rather than the extent of smiling, influences the customer's emotions and perceptions."

However, another study[3] of male and female participants buying stereos from male and female salespeople had more ambiguous results. This time, researchers found that male prospects were slightly more likely to buy from a smiling versus neutral female sales clerk but slightly less likely to buy from a smiling versus neutral male sales clerk. Female prospects, on the other hand, remained unaffected by smiles, regardless of the salesperson's gender.

If the research indicates that smiling does not matter, or at least matters only under select conditions, then you're probably wondering why "smile" is one of our 12 habits. Smiling projects a positive attitude that you feel on the inside and people see on the outside. Selling is hard work filled with a few shining moments in an otherwise vast ocean of rejection. Our best advice is to project a positive outlook and view the journey as the reward. Smiling is also code for rapport building. Our research, including the two studies discussed above, was conducted in synthetic, high-transactional, business-to-consumer settings. In the business-to-business world, it is generally accepted (though not scientifically proven, to our knowledge) that there is a strong relationship between trust and the propensity to purchase and renew.

6. Ask

It is written that great salespeople are great listeners, and we have no reason to doubt this. In fact, it makes perfect sense. We were curious, however, if academic studies actually supported this, so we did some research.

In the first study[4] we found, researchers sent a mail survey to 500 new car buyers and received 173 usable responses. The questionnaire explored 13 components of listening in addition to 4 that assessed trust, 3 that assessed customer satisfaction, and 4 that assessed future willingness to interact with the salesperson. That study found that listening was positively related to both trusting in and to willingness to interact with that salesperson in the future. Listening was not significantly correlated with satisfaction as measured by three understandably unrelated factors: "amount of contact," "level of service," and "dealings with this salesperson."

Although that first study convinced us of the link between listening and trust in transactional B2C environments, we went deeper because we needed to know the connection between listening and performance in a relational B2B environment. So we kept digging.

We found a second study[5] in which researchers asked for and received 79 self-assessments from the salespeople of a Fortune 100 international electronics manufacturer while they were attending a company-sponsored training program. The questionnaire had 16 items measuring adaptive selling behaviors, 8 items measuring job satisfaction, and 8 items measuring job performance. One additional item, "My customers probably consider me to be a good listener," was also positively correlated with all three categories. In particular, the correlation between listening and performance was 0.337, indicating that 11.4 percent (r squared) of the variation in self-assessed performance was explained by variation in self-assessed listening ability.

In case you are worried that the self-assessment was biased, other studies[6] have shown that the technique is accurate when conducted carefully. Nevertheless, we turned to a third study,[7] so as not to have even a lingering shadow of doubt. This final study consisted of examining pairs of financial advisors and clients. Ultimately, there was a total of 778 usable responses from clients and 418 from advisors working for 10 different finan-cial institutions. Though nominally B2C, this study took into consideration almost everything we had hoped for: (1) it used quantitative performance data supplied by employers, (2) it was based on customer assessment rather than self-assessment of lis-tening ability, and (3) it was based on a sales process that was highly relationship oriented. Even after adjusting for age, gender, education, and experience, this study found a significant "positive association between customers' perceptions of the salesperson's listening effectiveness and the salesperson's quantitative sales performance."

Most academic studies deconstruct listening into the three main areas of sensing, evaluating, and responding. These areas, along with their supporting subcomponents, show in detail how the significant drivers of performance actually work:

1. Sensing
   - Focus on the prospect by avoiding outside interrup-tions from people or machines (e-mails, phone calls, text messages, and so on).
   - Maintain firm and appropriate eye contact.
   - Exhibit and read nonverbal gestures such as head nods.
   - Take notes.

2. Evaluating
   - Understand the client's or prospect's point of view, concerns, and needs by asking for more details with probing, clarifying, and continuing questions.
   - Paraphrase and/or reformulate the client's or prospect's questions.
   - Do not interrupt the client or prospect. Answer only at appropriate times.
   - Stay on the subject.

3. Responding
   - Use full sentences instead of one-word responses like "yes" or "no."
   - Offer information relevant to questions asked.
   - Show genuine interest and enthusiasm.

7. Respond

Follow up rapidly and efficiently on inquiries and requests from prospects and clients.

Professional Effectiveness

8. Record

Rather than viewing CRM as a necessary administrative evil, embrace it as a critical ally in growing your business (and your bank account) by building and maintaining relationships with clients and prospects. To that end, keep contacts up to date, capture detailed notes, and set tasks and reminders.

9. Persist and Personalize

Persistence pays. Whether the number of touches needed to set meetings is 8 or 10 or 20, the frequency is certainly higher than the mere 1 or 2 that most salespeople attempt. Keep touches delicate and personalized so that they do not become an annoyance. "Delicate" means not leaving a voice mail after every call or not calling an excessive number of times over too short an amount of time.

Personalize means that *every* e-mail, voice mail, phone conversation, and live meeting demonstrates and reflects that you did precall planning and came prepared with background and context.

10. Expand

As Aaron Ross mentioned in his foreword, salespeople routinely fall into a vicious trap. They start out as strong business developers until their book of business is large enough to slip into account management mode for ease and comfort. They renew existing business rather than finding new business.

To break that cycle, the highest-performing salespeople maintain an expansion mindset. They ask existing customers for warm referrals into other parts of their business. The best time to ask for a referral is the point at which you have concluded that the prospects are truly not interested. Finally, pay it forward by providing referrals to others; in most instances, reciprocity will kick in, and they will repay the favor; if not, you will at least have accrued some good karma.

11. Protect

Especially in today's information age, guard your reputation as your most valuable selling asset. If you do not feel the particular sales approach that management is asking you to execute is appropriate, then speak up. If they do not listen, find another job with an employer who understands that the strength of their business is based on the reputations of their employees.

12. Learn

You have reached the end of this book, which proves you have embraced the last and most important habit of highly successful sales development representatives—continuous learning. To be successful and to stay that way, you need to constantly maintain your competitive edge by perpetually sharpening your skills in every one of the following areas:

- Customer knowledge

- Product knowledge

- Competitive knowledge

- Sales process knowledge

- Interpersonal skills, especially communications

The Future of Predictable Prospecting

Prognostications of a dramatically different future of selling are a dime a dozen. Many so-called experts contend that companies should retool to become 100 percent inbound. They argue that by combining content creation and marketing automation, salespeople can just sit back and wait for high quality leads to land on their laps. Other pundits say that salespeople need not use the phone or e-mail for prospecting; rather, they can rely on social selling via platforms like Twitter, LinkedIn, and Facebook to get the job done.

We feel certain that those two futures are not *our* future. Sales is, always has been, and always will be about hustle. Yes, for brief periods of time, a B2B product or service may be so compelling that a great living can be made from inbound leads alone. However, savvy competitors ensure that nirvana will not last long. By the same token, a social-selling-only world is a pipe dream. Prospects use social media to build and maintain relationships, and they will abandon platforms that get too sales-y.

Current trends suggest a medium-term future that makes selling a little easier. The changes we anticipate include the following:

- Data-driven tools that make it easier to develop and evolve Ideal Account Profiles (IAPs) and Ideal Prospect Personas (IPPs)

- Far more accurate databases that can be used for identifying leads matching an IAP and IPP

- Intra- and possibly inter-company knowledge bases of which practices are working and which are not working such as touch type and frequency, and e-mail language

- Account-based selling tools that make personalization more painless

We want to leave you with the thought we started with: open-mindedness. Always be testing. It is the surest way to winning a sale.

Happy Predictable Prospecting!

APPENDIX

Quick Guide to Predictable Prospecting

In this book, we explain the what, why, and how of countless immediately actionable best practices and templates designed to make your prospecting predictable. However, we recognize that many readers, particularly sales development professionals, crave a quick summary, especially of our advice on crafting messaging and designing multitouch, multichannel campaigns.

To address this need, this appendix demonstrates how one of us (Marylou, an independent sales process consultant) would apply the framework to engage the other (Jeremey, a sales operations leader at a midsized information services company).

Step 1. Build a Six-Factor SWOT Analysis

Marylou must have a strong understanding of why prospects should buy from her rather than from the competition to position her sales process consulting services successfully.

To express her differentiated value propositions, she constructs a SWOT (strengths, weaknesses, opportunities, and threats) analysis consisting of the 4 Ps (product, price, promotion, and place); reputation and internal resources; external forces; trends; and VUCA (volatile, uncertain, complex, and ambiguous) factors. Boiling down her analysis to the three to five highest-impact factors, Marylou produces the SWOT analysis in Table A-1.

TABLE A-1 SWOT Analysis for Marylou's Sales Strategy Consultancy

STRENGTHS	WEAKNESSES	OPPORTUNITIES	THREATS
1. Tenure, expertise, track record in outbound prospecting (25+ years); credentials (author, speaker, lecturer). 2. Blend of technical (engineering) and sales acumen; tactical frameworks with actionable metrics. 3. Conversion rate optimization expertise (intra- and inter-sales stage metrics, e-mail copy, content assets).	1. Only one person: cannot service more than 5 accounts per quarter. 2. Decision to stay focused on cold outreach can be limiting. 3. Price: no programs or services other than mentoring and coaching; cannot help solo entrepreneurs.	1. Launch outbound prospecting optimization agency. 2. License workshop for one-to-many instruction. 3. Create professional certification programs.	1. Market decides cold outreach is no longer needed. 2. No legacy in place: when Marylou retires, so does the knowledge. 3. Buyer behavior and psychology radically change due to changing technology and prospect preferences.

Step 2. Develop an Ideal Account Profile (IAP)

The ideal accounts for Marylou to target in an outbound prospecting campaign are those that not only value her differentiation (from Step 1) but also offer the maximum return on effort, vis-à-vis a high likelihood of buying and a high lifetime value. Considering firmographic, operational, and situational factors, she constructs the IAP in Figure A-1.

FIGURE A-1	**IAP for Campaign Targeting Information Services Companies**
FIRMOGRAPHIC	• Companies with direct sales forces (internal or partner channels) • Revenue between $250 million and $2 billion • United States and global: major cities
OPERATIONAL	• Frustrated with inconsistent sales prospecting process • Unable to generate qualified opportunities consistently and predictably • Don't know what metrics to measure or when or how to measure them
SITUATIONAL	• Sales leadership transition • Specializing sales roles • Entering new market; launching new product

Step 3. Craft an Ideal Prospect Persona (IPP)

In Step 2, Marylou identified the right companies to target. Now she needs to determine the right types of people. She does this with the help of the Ideal Prospect Persona (IPP) shown in Table A-2.

TABLE A-2	IPP for Sales Operations Professionals
Target functions and seniority	Chief revenue officer; VP or director of sales operations or sales strategy; director of marketing, new business.
Professional objectives	1. Increase sales productivity as measured by average revenue per associate (by tenure band). 2. Increase sales engagement as measured by employee retention rate (by tenure band).
Influence map	1. Direct influencers: line-of-business leaders and sales leaders, as well as cross-functional partners in human resources, product management, customer service, and marketing. 2. Gatekeepers: administrative assistants, corporate counsels, risk managers, and internal finance professionals. 3. Indirect influencers: talent development peers; product engineering and individual sales professionals.
Core value proposition	1. Why change? Current outbound prospecting (the status quo) is not predictably delivering sufficient pipeline. 2. Why now? To meet annual targets for sales productivity and sales engagement. 3. Why with me? Track record of designing, delivering, and implementing predictable prospecting playbooks.

Step 4. Craft Compelling Messaging

Crafting messaging that helps the seller identify where the prospect is in her buying journey is one of the central tenets of the Predictable Prospecting methodology. To that end, Marylou constructs the following prospecting e-mails:

- From unaware to aware (see Figure A-2)

- From aware to interested (see Figure A-3)

- From interested to evaluating (see Figure A-4)

- Breakup and referral (see Figure A-5)

- From evaluating to purchase (see Figure A-6)

Additionally, the e-mails demonstrate taking a highly personalized approach to prospecting, which is increasingly necessary.

| FIGURE A-2 | **Unaware to Aware Prospecting E-mail** |

From: <Marylou's_e-mail_address>

Subject: Congrats

Jeremey,

Congrats on your new job as head of sales strategy at GLG. Assuming you'll be ramping up outbound efforts, I thought you'd find this article I wrote helpful. It covers seven "quick wins" in your first 100 days leading sales ops:

Sales Operations Leadership: Your First 100 Days

I hope this is helpful. Good luck and much success in your new position. I'm sure you'll make quite an impact on the company. Don't hesitate to reach out if you need something.

(continued)

Thank you,

Marylou

<Marylou's_full_e-mail_signature>

P.S.: I came up with a new strategy after I wrote the article that several sales ops leaders I work with have successfully implemented. Do you want to kick the idea around? I'm free next Tuesday, February 9, at 10 a.m., for a quick chat if that works for you.

FIGURE A-3   Aware to Interested Prospecting E-mail

From: <Marylou's_e-mail_address>

Subject: Re: Congrats

Jeremey,

I noticed on LinkedIn that we are mutually connected to <mutual_contact_name>. I love her book <book_title>. Don't you?

By the way, I recently created a Sales Operations Maturity Assessment that I'd love to share with you. Clients have told me they find it particularly valuable for ramping up their new prospect engagement capabilities.

The tool helps size up your organization's maturity based on seven categories: orientation, management and leadership, organizational alignment, technology, budget and staffing, analytics, and sales process.

If it's something you'd be interested in, let me know and I'll send it over.

(continued)

Thank you,

Marylou

<Marylou's_full_e-mail_signature>

P.S.: Are you settling in yet at <prospect_company>? Did you know <some_interesting_tidbit_about_the_prospect's_ company>?

<Include_text_of_original_e-mail_since_this_is_a_reply.>

FIGURE A-4 **Interested to Evaluating Prospecting E-mail**

<BOXT>From: <Marylou's_e-mail_address>

Subject: Personal Invitation

Jeremey,

I just went back to GLG's website and noticed you added video testimonials featuring customers talking about their experiences with your professional learning platform. Very cool.

I'm hosting a private call next Wednesday, February 17, for my best clients and prospects to discuss recent changes to their sales compensation models. The discussion is limited to eight sales ops VPs from $250 million to $2 billion companies. I have two slots left and invite you to attend as my personal guest.

Just reply with a time you are able to chat, and I'll call you to provide the details.

Best,

Marylou

<Marylou's_full_e-mail_signature>

FIGURE A-5 **Breakup and Referral Prospecting E-mail**

From: <Marylou's_e-mail_address>

Subject: Re: Should I Contact <Prospect's_Colleague>?

Jeremey,

I have been trying to connect with you over the past two weeks to explore ways I can partner with you to increase sales productivity at GLG. Since I have not heard back from you, I'm left to draw a few possible conclusions:

1. You are all set with sales productivity partners, and if that is the case, please reply with "1" so that I stop bothering you.

2. You are interested in a partnership, but you are just very busy right now. If this is the case, please reply with "2."

3. You see opportunity but <prospect's_colleague> is a better contact for these topics. If that is the case, please reply with "3" and cc her.

Please advise,

Marylou

<Marylou's_full_e-mail_signature>

Note: The evaluating to purchase e-mail in Figure A-6 assumes that Marylou is well down the sales cycle with Jeremey.

FIGURE A-6	**Evaluating to Purchase Prospecting E-mail**

From: <Marylou's_e-mail_address>

Subject: Regarding the Reference You Requested

Jeremey,

I am enjoying getting to know you.

To recap, I understand you are looking for a partner to help you achieve your primary annual objective: increasing average revenue per rep by <percentage> this calendar year.

As requested, I have set up a call for you with <reference_name> on Friday, February 26, at 2 p.m. EST. Here are the dial-in details: <phone and access code>. I will reach out to you as discussed at 3 p.m. to see how things went and to discuss next steps.

Thank you,

Marylou

<Marylou's_full_e-mail_signature>

Step 5. Design a Multitouch, Multichannel Cadence

With messaging in hand, Marylou next designs a multitouch, multichannel cadence designed to secure an introductory meeting with Jeremey. Her cadence, illustrated in Table A-3, relies on e-mails and phone calls.

TABLE A-3	Outbound Campaign with Nine Touches in 16 Business Days

DAY	TOUCH TYPE	CONTENT	CALL TO ACTION
1	E-mail (1)	First 100 days	Unaware to aware asset download
1	Call with voice mail (1)	None	Secure meeting
4	Call with no voice mail (2)	None	Secure meeting
7	E-mail (2)	Maturity assessment	Aware to interested link request
7	Call with no voice mail (3)	None	Secure meeting
10	Call with no voice mail (4)	None	Secure meeting
13	E-mail (3)	Best-practices call	Accept interested to evaluating call invite
13	Call with voice mail (5)	None	Reply to e-mail (3)
16	E-mail (4)	Breakup	Referral to colleague

Step 6. Attempt to (Dis-)Qualify Prospects

Assuming Marylou secures a first meeting with Jeremey, she should work to determine, Are we a fit (AWAF)? AWAF works both ways since it is not only important for the prospect to see value but it is also critical for the salesperson to weed out (disqualify) prospects who are either unlikely to buy or unlikely to realize value after they buy. To accomplish this, Marylou must apply the must-have operational and situational criteria she established in the Ideal Account Profile (IAP from Step 2). To recap:

- Frustrated with inconsistent sales prospecting process

- Unable to generate sales qualified opportunities consistently and predictably

- Don't know what metrics to measure, when to measure, and how to measure

- Sales leadership transition

- Separation of sales roles; no business development process in place

- New market, new product, or new vertical to deploy in outreach channel

With AWAF completed, she can progress through more traditional opportunity qualification. The Predictable Prospecting framework relies on a resequencing of BANT into the following order: need, timing, authority, and budget. At a minimum, Marylou plans to ask Jeremey the following:

- *Need:* What are your primary performance objectives? How do you rank each in terms of importance?

- *Timing:* Where does improving sales productivity rank in your overall priorities?

- *Authority:* In addition to you, who else in your organization is responsible for improving sales productivity?

- *Budget:* How is funding for a project like this determined?

Step 7. Block Time for Prospecting

This book contains many frameworks for successful prospecting. But all of them will fail unless you set and adhere to daily calendar blocks dedicated to prospecting. For full-time sales development reps, we recommend four 90-minute slots. Table A-4 provides a recommended daily calendar for a full-time sales development representative with a daily goal of five to six hours of uninterrupted prospecting time.

TABLE A-4	Recommended Daily Calendar for Full-Time Sales Development Representative
08:00–08:30	Set 3 goals, and review plan for the day.
08:30–09:30	Handle e-mail responses. Update CRM.
09:30–10:00	Personal time (15 minutes). Plan first call session.
10:00–12:00	Phone prospecting with the goal of setting at least 1 meeting (allow no interruptions).
12:00–01:00	Lunch and personal time.
01:00–02:00	Qualification calls (or additional phone prospecting).
02:00–03:00	E-mail and social prospecting (allow no interruptions).
03:00–03:30	Personal time (15 minutes). Plan second call session.
03:30–05:30	Phone prospecting with the goal of setting at least 1 meeting (allow no interruptions).
05:30–06:00	Handle e-mail responses. Prepare plan for next day.

NOTES

Foreword

1. http://www.inc.com/matt-cooper/how-silicon-valley-sells.html.

Chapter 1

1. http://www.gartner.com/newsroom/id/3056118.
2. Robert P. Desisto and Tad Travis, "Magic Quadrant for Sales Force Automation," Gartner, July 9, 2015.
3. Ibid.
4. Ibid.
5. Fiscal year ending January 31, 2015.
6. *United Breaks Guitars*, https://www.youtube.com/watch?v=5YGc4zOqozo.
7. Net Promoter Score (NPS) is a trademark of Bain & Company, Fred Reichheld, and Satmetrix.
8. http://www.temkingroup.com/research-reports/net-promoter-score-benchmark-study-2014/.
9. https://experiencematters.wordpress.com/2012/05/14/net-promoter-score-and-market-share-for-60-tech-vendors/.
10. https://experiencematters.wordpress.com/2013/05/28/report-tech-vendor-nps-benchmark-2013/.
11. https://experiencematters.wordpress.com/2014/07/30/report-tech-vendor-nps-benchmark-2014/.
12. http://www.intellectualventures.com/news/press-releases/intellectual-ventures-announces-patent-agreement-with-salesforce.com.
13. Michael Porter, Nicholas Argyres, and Anita M. McGahan, "An Interview with Michael Porter," *Academy of Management Executive*, vol. 16, no. 2, p. 44.

Chapter 2

1. http://www.seattletimes.com/business/boeing-celebrates-787-delivery-as-programs-costs-top-32-billion/.
2. The Boeing Company 2014 annual report.

3. The Boeing Company, U.S. SEC Form 8-K, June 22, 2015.

Chapter 3

1. https://www.trainingindustry.com/sales-training/top-company-listings/2015/2015-top-20-sales-training-companies.aspx.
2. http://www.nytimes.com/2015/05/09/business/media/as-spotify-expands-revenue-rises-and-losses-deepen.html.

Chapter 4

1. Ian Davis et al., *The McKinsey Approach to Problem Solving*, McKinsey Staff Paper 727940, 2007.
2. "Compel with Content" is a trademark of Marylou Tyler. The "For whom . . . To do what . . . In order to . . . By what means . . ." approach is the intellectual property of Jeremey Donovan.
3. http://mailchimp.com/resources/research/e-mail-marketing-subject-line-comparison/.
4. http://returnpath.com/wp-content/uploads/2015/04/RP-Subject-Line-Report-FINAL.pdf.
5. http://blog.mailchimp.com/subject-line-data-choose-your-words-wisely/.
6. http://www.mailermailer.com/resources/metrics/2012/summary.rwp.
7. This is actually from another MailChimp resource: http://kb.mailchimp.com/campaigns/previews-and-tests/best-practices-for-email-subject-lines.
8. https://marketing.grader.com/.

Chapter 5

1. http://static.insidesales.com/assets/pdf/a-five-year-retrospective-the-original-lead-response-management-study.pdf and https://hbr.org/2011/03/the-short-life-of-online-sales-leads.
2. http://mailchimp.com/resources/research/email-marketing-benchmarks/.
3. Required win rate = <cost × (1 + ROI)> / <(lifetime value) × (number of leads)>.
4. Nielsen, "Global Trust in Advertising and Brand Messages," September 2013, http://www.nielsen.com/content/dam/corporate/us/en/reports-downloads/2013%20Reports/Nielsen-Global-Trust-in-Advertising-Report-September-2013.pdf.

5. https://www.implisit.com/blog/b2b-sales-benchmarks/.
6. Daniel Kahneman, "Evaluation by Moments, Past and Future." In Daniel Kahneman and Amos Tversky, *Choices, Values, and Frames,* Cambridge University Press, Cambridge, U.K., 2000, p. 693, ISBN 978-0521627498.
7. http://salesstaff.com/market-research-survey/.
8. http://static.insidesales.com/assets/pdf/ebook-the-art-of-cold -calling-and-the-science-of-contact-ratios.pdf.
9. The term *pattern interrupt* appears to have evolved from the oft-maligned field of neuro-linguistic programming (NLP). The first known use of the precise phrase in print was by Kerry L. Johnson in the 1988 book *Mastering the Game: The Human Edge in Sales and Marketing.* The phrase became highly popular soon after when it was adopted by Tony Robbins in a number of his books and seminars.
10. Kyle Porter, CEO of SalesLoft, in a private meeting at the Rainmaker 2016 conference.

Chapter 6

1. Netcraft September 2015 Web Server Study, http://news.netcraft .com/archives/2015/09/16/september-2015-web-server-survey .html.
2. Data.com, a Salesforce.com company, slides reprinted with permission. We removed certain slides (including but not limited to the company's safe harbor statement) and reordered and recolored (to grayscale) the remaining slides.
3. We were not able to verify that IBM coined the term "budget, authority, need, and timing (BANT)" despite many references to that effect.
4. SPIN Selling was created by Neil Rackham, founder of the sales training and consulting firm Huthwaite International, and author of the bestselling book *SPIN Selling.*

Chapter 7

1. http://www.silverpop.com/Documents/Whitepapers/2015/E-mail -Marketing-Metrics-Benchmark-Study-2015-Silverpop.pdf.
2. Ibid.
3. http://blog.vorsightbp.com/effective-cold-calling-the-power-of -direct-lines.

Chapter 9

1. Trish Bertuzzi, *Sales Development Rep (SDR) 2014 Metrics and Compensation*, Bridge Group, Inc., Hudson, MA, 2014.

2. Anat Rafaeli, Ori Hadomi, and Tal Simons, "Recruiting Through Advertising or Employee Referrals: Costs, Yields, and the Effects of Geographic Focus," *European Journal of Work and Organizational Psychology*, vol. 14, no. 4, 2005, pp. 355–366.

3. Michael G. Aamodt and Kimberly Carr, "The Relationship Between Recruitment Source and Employee Behavior," Proceedings of the Annual Meeting of the International Personnel Management Association Assessment Council, 1988, Las Vegas, Nevada, p. 151.

4. Jim Dickie and Barry Trailer, "Sales Management Optimization Study," *CSO Insights*, 2014.

5. Frank L. Schmidt and John E. Hunter, "The Validity and Utility of Selection Methods in Personnel Psychology: Practical and Theoretical Implications of 85 Years of Research Findings," *Psychological Bulletin*, vol. 124, no. 2, 1998, pp. 262–274.

6. Murray R. Barrick, Michael K. Mount, and Judy P. Strauss, "Conscientiousness and Performance of Sales Representatives: Test of the Mediating Effects of Goal Setting," *Journal of Applied Psychology*, vol. 78, no. 5, 1993, p. 715.

7. Willem Verbeke, Bart Dietz, and Ernst Verwaal, "Drivers of Sales Performance: A Contemporary Meta-Analysis: Have Salespeople Become Knowledge Brokers?" *Journal of the Academy of Marketing Science*, vol. 39, no. 3, 2011, pp. 407–428.

8. http://www.agsalesworks.com/blog-sales-prospecting -perspectives/5-reasons-not-to-build-your-sales-development -team-one-rep-at-a-time.

9. Bertuzzi, *Sales Development Rep (SDR) 2014 Metrics and Compensation*.

10. Ibid.

11. Ibid.

12. Ibid.

13. Timothy A. Judge and Joyce E. Bono, "Relationship of Core Self-evaluations Traits—Self-esteem, Generalized Self-efficacy, Locus of Control, and Emotional Stability—with Job Satisfaction and Job Performance: A Meta-Analysis," *Journal of Applied Psychology*, vol. 86, no. 1, 2001, p. 80.

Chapter 10

1. Eileen Wood et al., "Examining the Impact of Off-Task Multi-tasking with Technology on Real-Time Classroom Learning," *Computers & Education,* vol. 58, no. 1, 2012, pp. 365–374.

2. Thorsten Hennig-Thurau et al., "Are All Smiles Created Equal? How Emotional Contagion and Emotional Labor Affect Service Relationships," *Journal of Marketing,* vol. 70, no. 3, 2006, pp. 58–73.

3. M. H. Abel and M. Abel, "The Effects of a Sales Clerk's Smile on Consumer Perceptions and Behaviors," *American Journal of Psychological Research,* vol. 3, no. 1, 2007, pp. 17–28.

4. Rosemary P. Ramsey and Ravipreet S. Sohi, "Listening to Your Customers: The Impact of Perceived Salesperson Listening Behavior on Relationship Outcomes," *Journal of the Academy of Marketing Science,* vol. 25, no. 2, 1997, pp. 127–137.

5. Shepherd, C. David, Stephen B. Castleberry, and Rick E. Ridnour, "Linking Effective Listening with Salesperson Performance: An Exploratory Investigation," *Journal of Business & Industrial Marketing,* vol. 12, no. 5, 1997, pp. 315–322.

6. Jiing-Lih Farh, James D. Werbel, and Arthur G. Bedeian, "An Empirical Investigation of Self-Appraisal Based Performance Evaluation," *Academy of Management Proceedings,* vol. 41, no. 1, 1988; G. Churchill et al., "The Determinants of Salesperson Performance: A Meta-Analysis," *Journal of Marketing Research,* May 1985, pp. 103–108; and Douglas N. Behrman and William D. Perreault, "Measuring the Performance of Industrial Salespersons," *Journal of Business Research,* vol. 10, no. 3, 1982, pp. 355–370.

7. Jasmin Bergeron and Michel Laroche, "The Effects of Perceived Salesperson Listening Effectiveness in the Financial Industry," *Journal of Financial Services Marketing,* vol. 14, no. 1, 2009, pp. 6–25.

INDEX

ABOUT THE AUTHORS

Marylou Tyler is the founder of Strategic Pipeline, an outbound sales process improvement consulting group serving the Fortune 1000. Her client list includes prestigious companies such as Apple, Bose, AMA, talentd, CIBC, Prudential, UPS, Orkin, AAA, and MasterCard. She is also the coauthor of the Number 1 bestseller *Predictable Revenue: Turn Your Business into a Sales Machine with the $100 Million Best Practices of Salesforce.com*. In 2016, Marylou was nominated to the *20 Women to Watch in Sales Lead Management* list. A renowned sales process improvement expert, author, and engaging speaker, Marylou's proven processes help B2B businesses and sales teams maximize revenues and opportunities by optimizing their sales pipeline. To find out more, visit MarylouTyler.com.

Jeremey Donovan is SVP of sales strategy at Gerson Lehrman Group (GLG), the world's largest membership network for one-on-one professional learning. Previously, Jeremey was the chief marketing officer and senior vice president of sales at American Management Association (AMA) International. Prior to joining AMA, Jeremey served as the group vice president of marketing at Gartner Inc., the world's leading information technology research and advisory company. Jeremey is the author of six books, including the international public speaking bestseller *How to Deliver a TED Talk*. He holds a BS and an MS in electrical engineering from Cornell University and an MBA from the University of Chicago Booth School of Business.